Chaplaincy Ministry

Serving Christ Through Serving Others

Written and Compiled

By

Dr. Stan DeKoven

Chaplaincy Ministry
Serving Christ Through Serving Others

by Dr. Stan DeKoven

Copyright © 2018 By Stan DeKoven

ISBN 978-1-61529-210-3

For information on reordering, please contact:

Vision Publishing

P.O. Box 1680

Ramona, CA 92065

(760) 789-4700

www.booksbyvision.org

All rights in this book are reserved worldwide. No part of the book may be reproduced in any manner without the written permission of the author except in brief quotations embodied in critical articles or reviews.

Table of Contents

Acknowledgements v
Introduction vii
Vision Statement ix
Mission Statement xi
Statement of Faith xiii
The Chaplain's Creed xv
1. A Basic Theology of Chaplaincy Ministry 1
2. History of the Christian Church and Chaplaincy 5
3. What is a Chaplain? 13
4. Hospital Chaplaincy 17
5. Chaplaincy in the Justice System 29
6. The Chaplain in Prisons 37
7. Theology of Prison Ministry 45
8. Post Prison Ministry 71
9. The Chaplain's Role in Situations of Abuse 97
10. The Chaplain as Counselor 107
APPENDIX 115

Acknowledgements

We would like to thank our contributing authors for their assistance in the creation of this manual.

Dr. John Delgado, Dr. Stan DeKoven, Dr. Pat Hulsey and Dr. Kathy Smith have all significantly contributed to making the completion of this work possible.

Introduction

Welcome to a most exciting adventure!

There are many opportunities offered men and women to share their faith in Christ and minister his grace. Children and young people are generally the most open to the gospel, followed by men and women in life crises (divorce, death, etc.) One other group of men and women where there is an incredible opportunity to share the Great Commission with great compassion occurs as we care for those either hospitalized or incarcerated. It is often in the chaotic arena of hospital or prison chaplaincy that great Kingdom work can be done for the least of these, our brothers and sisters.

In this introductory and comprehensive course, an overview of Christ centered chaplaincy ministry will be presented. It is comprehensive while introductory and assumes that we are teaching:

- Mature Believers
- Recommended by their spiritual bodies
- With a heart to give dynamic care to the whosoever in need of chaplaincy services.

We believe you will find our course both instructive and inspirational with a goal of helping men and women become whole; spirit, soul and body.

Along with this text book, you have or will be provided a CD or link to the online lecture provided by one of our instructors, Dr. Stan DeKoven. Follow the PowerPoint and complete the required assignments to complete the requirements of the course.

Vision Statement

Vision International Training and Education Network (VITEN) resources institutions and organizations that serve the community, through training, education and literature, in partnership with Vision International University.

VISION seeks to develop healthy relationships with churches, communities, institutions, prisons and hospitals, and government organizations in order to provide education and training for local ministers who will be empowered to provide spiritual guidance to those who are experiencing various crises.

VISION partners with local churches in their role to guide individuals and families in the development of a positive relationship with God as Creator, Savior and Lord.

VISION serves with local churches to guide individuals and families to build positive relationships with others.

VISION equips men and women who have a heart to relieve pain and suffering by helping those in need, helping the least among us to recognize that they are important and loved by God and caregivers, who have been properly trained and been commissioned for this task.

Mission Statement

VISION is a ministry that seeks to train and equip ministers and lay people to serve the underserved in places such as hospitals, foster homes, correctional facilities, shelters, rehabilitation facilities, police stations, local communities; any place where need and crisis meets.

VISION seeks to prepare individuals committed to a life of service, the proclamation of the Gospel of Jesus Christ, according to the Scriptures, and have the calling to work as Volunteer Chaplains.

VISION seeks to relieve the pain and suffering, by helping individuals recognize that they are important and loved.

Statement of Faith

- We believe in the principles outlined in the Apostles' Creed.
- We believe in the dignity of the individual and that each individual has the right to live an abundant life.
- We believe that a person can find peace, healing and abundant life through a relationship with God as Creator, Savior and Lord.
- We believe we have the responsibility to bring the message of Good News of Jesus Christ to all, as stated in Matthew 28, the Great Commission.
- We believe in the redemptive work of Jesus Christ and the power to restore men and women through the ministry of the Holy Spirit.
- Vision also partners with Cornerstone Institute in Colorado Springs for students wanting to become full time paid chaplains for hospitals and other institutions. For more information, see the back of this book regarding opportunities for further study.

The Chaplain's Creed

- Lord you have called me to serve as chaplain in the same way you did with St. Martin of Tours. I know that you favor me, Lord, and I'm ready to serve.
- Lord, please help me, by providing me the ability to be sensitive to all and bless me with wisdom to find meaning in the ministry as I serve people in crisis.
- As Chaplain, I need your support to be a professional, with the ability to interact in difficult situations, giving others my best on your behalf.
- Bless me with the gift of listening, the art of counseling and the ability to support those in need.
- Please Lord, let me always be true to you, be accountable to your Word, be sensitive and respect the faith of others as I support individuals of other beliefs.
- Lord, let me be a shepherd for all and bless me when I confront evil forces.
- Lord, grant me the ability to reflect and contemplate on the meaning of events in my life and the lives of others. Give me the ability to work with common ideals and grant me the wisdom to understand, and love without judgment. Then I can provide care with confidence, love, responsibility and justice.
- Lord, bless me with the ability to create bridges where unity prevails instead of human differences.
- Let my life reflect Christ, in word and action, with compassion towards all I serve.
- Help me to accept people where they are, regardless their stage of human development, and not impose my beliefs on others.
- Dear Father, give me the strength and wisdom to recognize that many do not possess the miraculous knowledge that you exist.
- In the name of the Father, Son and Holy Spirit Amen!

1
A Basic Theology of Chaplaincy Ministry

Perhaps the best definition of an evangelical view of chaplaincy ministry was presented in "Blogging Chaplaincy" by Ruth Bradford http://chaplainsblogstargate2010.blogspot.com/2010/07/theology-of-chaplaincy.html

Sunday, July 18, 2010; Theology of Chaplaincy

Introduction

Chaplaincy in various settings is a vital and significant Christian ministry. This unique calling takes on many forms within each unique setting, whether prison, nursing home, public or private health care institution, athletic organization, etc. While there are many models of Chaplaincy developed, each with their own Biblical theology and philosophy of ministry supporting them, each setting in which Chaplaincy takes place is unique. Though models can change, and places of service can be quite divergent, our basic philosophy and theology needs to be firmly grounded in scripture to be effective in our work.

Ideally, the chaplain needs to have a strong theological framework in which the practical aspects of Chaplaincy can be worked out, while making use of one's experience, skills, talents, and passions. This is ultimately the foundation for the particular and potent chaplains' ministry. Much of what chaplaincy becomes for an individual is formed by his or her theology of ministry.

This chapter looks at the foundational issues of chaplaincy by discussing its origins and concludes with a biblical theology behind chaplaincy, which can and should be applied to whatever setting the chaplain finds him or herself in.

Origins of Chaplaincy

(more on this will be presented in Chapter 3)

Before looking at the practical and theological origins, aspects of chaplaincy as ministry and definition of the word and its usages would be helpful.

Etymology of the word *chaplain*

Origin: ME. chapele, OFr.1 chapele, capele, from ML cappella, LL. capella, dim. of cappa, a cope, cape; from the cappella or cloak of St. Martin of Tours preserved as a sacred relic in a chapel built for it; the cloak was preserved by the Frankish kings as a sacred relic, was borne before them in battle and used to give sanctity to oaths, and the name "chapel" (and variations) was applied to the sanctuary in which this cloak (cappa or cape) was preserved under the care of its cappellani or "chaplains"; thence "chapel" generally referred to a sanctuary containing holy relics, attached to a palace, etc., and so to any private sanctuary or holy place.

The term 'Chaplain' originates from the 4th Century St Martin of Tours, who was said to have cut his cape in half to give to a man in need while serving in the army. The relic of his cloak was preserved by the chaplains, and the term eventually came to mean those clergy who were 'made available to those who did not have free and frequent access [to church] like those who lived in town or a cathedral city. The services of Chaplains provided faith-based resources to those away from home and in foreign theatres, in the military, in hospitals and in prisons.' The origins of Chaplaincy lie with clergy who serve in institutions other than the church, originally in the army, but the modern view sees chaplaincy as a profession; a professional Christian working in a secular environment.

St. Martin's experience included a vision in which Jesus appeared to him saying "Martin, who is still but a catechumen, clothed me with this robe", which has similarities to the story found in Matthew 25:35-40 '35 "For I was hungry and you gave me something to eat, I was thirsty and you gave me something to drink, I was a stranger and you invited me in, I needed clothes and you clothed me, I was sick and you looked after me, I was in prison and you came to visit me.'" Then the righteous will answer him, 'Lord, when did we see you hungry and feed you, or thirsty and give you something to drink? When did we see you a stranger and invite you in, or needing clothes and clothe you? When did we see you sick or in prison and go to visit you?' The King will reply, "I tell you the truth, whatever you did for one of the least of these brothers of mine, you did for me."

This is one of the main scriptures underpinning chaplaincy (and should be for all ministry this side of the cross); the original meaning of the word and the story that goes with it is at the core of chaplaincy ministry, and provides an exhortation to care for people in need. We see from St Martin's example that we are to be a representative of Christ and the broader church, to those to whom we minister, highlighting the perspective that in God's view the way we treat other people is how we treat God himself. In caring for others, a Chaplain is to 'be like Christ.'

The Example of Christ

Although Jesus ministered in the synagogue at times, and in the temple in Jerusalem, his primary ministry activity took place in the marketplace…in homes, at the sides of a lake, as he went along the way. Jesus demonstrated the arriving Kingdom of God through his teaching, but more so through many miracles of healing. He often ministered most profoundly to the "common" man and woman in need…prostitutes, lepers, the daughters of leaders, etc. All during his ministry he was teaching his disciples, who would become apostles, to do as he did…heal the sick, raise the dead, cast out demons…freely received, freely give. (Matthew 10:8) Chaplains are motivated not by religious sentiment, but by genuine compassion, for the lost, needy, prisoners, widows and orphans, without judgment for how they came to their station in life. Thus, without judgment, Chaplains are to motivate in a similar vein, to reach out in care and comfort to "the least of these." (Matthew 25:40)

2

History of the Christian Church and Chaplaincy

You may be asking, what does this have to do with being a chaplain? Well, chaplains always work or serve within a certain context, and within culture. As citizens of a nation, such as the United States and a citizen of the Kingdom of God, we must operate from two perspectives and two mandates. First, and most important, we are loyal and faithful to the word of God. We are ministers of the Gospel of the Kingdom. Secondly, we must work under the mandates of the Constitution of the government where we reside and serve, and the various constitutions or legal authorities of the states and cities we serve in. Finally, we are accountable to the hospital, prison, or hospice we are serving in. Thus, a brief review (for sake of example, this must be adapted to the nation you find yourself serving in) of the US constitution. Of course, if you are studying this from another great nation, you should be aware of your specific ministry privileges and constraints. The history of chaplaincy, beginning in Europe, and extending to the United States, are a part of our church history, providing the background for chaplaincy ministry.

The (very brief) History of the Church in America

Introduction

Christianity is a religion based on the life and teachings of Jesus Christ. There are three major divisions making up the majority of church life around the world, and in the United States. They are:

1. The Protestant
2. The Catholic
3. The Greek Orthodox (Eastern)

Although there are differences in doctrine and practice, belief in Jesus Christ is the center for all of them.

Christians believe:

- There is only one God.
- He is the Creator and sustainer of the universe.
- He created mankind in his image and likeness and determined for mankind to rule and reign with him over the affairs of the world. Further, as a good Father, he continues to care for us.

Protestants, and especially evangelicals believe:

- In the proclamation of the gospel of Jesus Christ as revealed in the Bible.
- That the Bible is the true revelation of God and is authoritative in all it affirms.
- Though mankind was created without sin, man rebelled against the just law of God and thus sin entered the world, and thus all sin and are in need of a Savior.

The gospel message is summed up by one Bible verse:

"For God so loved the world that He gave His only begotten Son that whosoever believes in Him shall not perish but have everlasting life."

John 3:16

The doctrines of the Christian faith are based on the Word of God, summarized in 2 Timothy 3:16-17;

"All Scripture is inspired by God and profitable for teaching, for reproof, for correction, for training in righteousness; that the man of God may be adequate, equipped for every good work."

The Early Church

From the beginning of Jesus' ministry, his intention was to build the church of Jesus Christ through the preaching of the Kingdom of God. It is his church, and he is building it (Matthew 16:18). Chaplains are called and commissioned by Christ to participate in the proclamation of the good news of the Kingdom of God and in nurturing the faithful and assisting the unfaithful within the church and without. He began with John the Baptist.

- John the Baptist announced The Kingdom of God is at hand, "behold, the Lamb of God who takes away the sin of the world." (John 1:29)
- Jesus was a Jewish Rabbi who claimed and demonstrated himself to be the Messiah, the Son of God, the Savior of the world and God incarnate. He preached the good news of God's kingdom using parables and demonstrated the Kingdom through signs, wonders and miracles.
- His disciples (who later became apostles) continued his ministry and spread the gospel of the Kingdom to the known world
- This gospel has continued to be preached around the world; a movement called Christianity.

History of the Christian Church

- Christians were persecuted for over 250 years by various emperors until the year 313 AD.
- In that year, the Emperor Constantine gave Christians the freedom to practice their religion; a good and bad day for Christianity. Freedom to preach was a blessing, but under the sanctuary of the Emperor, and under the control of the Emperor, many problems of the movement occurred leading to the institutionalization of the movement.

- In 392 AD. Christianity became the official religion of the Roman Empire, and the period of rapid expansion of the religion occurred, and apostasies of the church also began.
- The church grew and spread far across the Western empire.
- During the Middle Ages, Christianity replaced the Roman Empire as a force that changed the world, but also had to endure the Dark Ages of the church. Where the early church was filled with wonders and miracles, martyrs and saints of great faith, the church as an institution become less vibrant, though never without a remnant of true believers.
- In 1456, Johann Gutenberg printed the Latin Vulgate, the first book printed with movable type, making the Bible accessible to more people.
- In 1517 the Protestant Reformation began when Martin Luther, a German monk, who criticized the Catholic Church for its indulgent practices, including the sale of indulgences (as a means of grace and door to heaven), nailed his 95 Theses (challenges or complaints for debate) on the Wittenberg church door.
- Other men such as John Wycliffe, John Calvin and William Tyndall helped shape the Reformation; an attempt to see the church returned to a more biblical faith.
- Luther and other men believed in justification by faith, which formed the foundation of Protestant beliefs:

1) Justification by faith, not by works - Ephesians 2:8-9
2) "Solo Scriptura or Only the Scriptures" - only the Bible dictates matters of Christian doctrine and not the church.
3) Separation of Church and State - Martin Luther did not believe the church should engage in politics. He only sought to instruct judges in spiritual matters. This is not

the same as it is practiced in the United States now, which is more separation for the church from being involved in the State, whereas the separation of Church and state doctrine in the United States was founded on the principle that there should be no official State religion, such as was the case in Europe at the time.

4) The priesthood of all believers - all believers have authority and thus responsibility. The layman has the duty to be active in all church affairs, including the government of the church, worship, and evangelism.

5) Only two sacraments - the only two sacraments which apply are: baptism and communion (The Lord's Supper). These are the only two that Jesus commanded us to observe.

From 1545 to 1563 there was a Counter-Reformation - The Council of Trent

The Catholic Church made significant reforms in response to the Protestant reformation. In fact, both the Catholic and Protestant branches of the church made, and continues to reform its' beliefs and practices, with a goal of returning to "pure" Christian faith. As an observer of history and participant in the life of the church, one can see many reforms still needed, and many controversies remain in the life of the church that Jesus is building.

The World and the Church

Through church history, there continued to be movement and discoveries that has challenged the church and its teachings. They include:

1800's Modern developments, Christianity, and Science

Charles Darwin and the "Survival of the Fittest," with his pseudo-scientific theory of evolution became a threat to many religious leaders, as they espoused an alternative explanation of the origin of the universe without God.

1900's Christianity and Technology

Many people wondered whether religion could meet human needs. As a result, many Christians responded by focusing on the problems of human welfare, world peace and human rights.

1948 The World Council of Churches

The ecumenical movement was formed to create unity between churches and denominations.

2000's Christianity and Philosophy

American Humanism takes root for many in place of traditional religion. Witchcraft and the New Age become accepted along with Christianity. Many new religions emerged in response to Biblical Christianity. In Europe, prior to the 20th century, most countries were Christian. Today only 1% of the population is Christian and one-tenth of 1% are evangelical Christians. Martyrdom of Christians continues to occur around the world, but the Kingdom of God continues to advance, especially amongst people of color and in the Southern Hemisphere.

The Church in America

1492

Columbus arrived with 12 priests and Baptist Ministers They built the first two churches on the North American continent, "St. Augustine" and "The First Baptist Church." Many came to the New World seeking religious freedom, along with those seeking fame and fortune.

1631

The Covenant of Virginia was made between Native Americans and the 13 Colonies, and for the first time Thanksgiving was celebrated. Of course, American leaders, like with many nations, often were better at making covenants than keeping them…just like the children of Israel of old. The marriage between John Smith and

Pocahontas exemplified the union between settlers and Native Americans.

1776

The Declaration of Independence. The 13 colonies declared independence from England as a protest of the influence of the British crown and a state religion. Thus, a new nation was born…not perfect, and not as actively Christian in practice and principle…but the principles were and are still a part of the history of America and its people, and hopefully will continue to be as the nation continues in the 21st Century.

The United States Constitution

1787, The Constitution of the United States was signed and ratified. The significance of this can be seen in the Constitution itself.

1. It sets out the fundamental laws of our nation's government.
2. Establishes the form of government that the people are to adhere to.
3. Defines the rights and freedoms of the American people (at least most, with unfortunate consequences for people of color and Native Americans).

The Preamble to the Constitution:

"We the People of the United States, in order to form a more perfect Union, establish Justice, insure domestic tranquility, provide for the common defense, promote the general welfare and secure the blessings of liberty to ourselves and our posterity do ordain and establish this constitution of the United States of America."

The Constitution consists of seven (7) articles and twenty-seven (27) amendments.

The first 10 amendments are known as "The Bill of Rights."

The First Amendment describes the five most important rights of a citizen:

1. Freedom of Religion
2. Freedom of Speech
3. Freedom of the Press
4. The right to peaceful assembly
5. The right to petition the government

These rights or freedoms allow us, as ministers of the Gospel, to freely practice and share our Christian faith, to speak freely within limits (more to follow below), to share our beliefs in writing, to gather for worship and instruction, and to express our complaints on behalf of ourselves and others, to seek justice as necessary. All are important for us as Christian caregivers in the work of Chaplaincy.

The fact is, all of our work as chaplains is done within the context of the history in which we share. The church in the United States, as in many Western nations, has the privilege and right to exercise our freedom in worship, and work within the constraints, at least at present, favorable of faith expression, not just in church but in the market place of ideas as well.

3

What is a Chaplain?

History and Definition of the Chaplain

As previously stated, the term "chaplain" comes to us from a fourth-century legend of St. Martin of Tours. St. Martin was a member of the Roman army who was born around 316 AD in Pannonia, [a Roman province including Hungary today] in a pagan family. At the age of approximately 21 years, a very cold day, he passed the gates of Amiens in Gaul (what is now France) and saw a man who was freezing at the roadside. Martin, moved by compassion after seeing and hearing the pleas of the beggar, decided to help. Martin took his most valuable possession, his coat, and cut it in half, giving the beggar one half and keeping the other half.

That night, the story continues, Martin had a vision in which he understood that the beggar was none other than Christ Himself! Martin's vision transformed his life. After this experience, he decided to follow the Christian faith and was baptized by Bishop Hillary. When he told this experience to others, the remaining half of his coat was kept as a relic and an object of value as a reminder of that event.

The origin of the word chaplain comes from this story, "mid-14c., "minister of a chapel," from Old French chapelein "clergyman" (Modern French chapelain), from Medieval Latin cappellanus "clergyman," originally "custodian of St. Martin's cloak" (see chapel). Replaced Old English capellane (from the same Medieval Latin source) "clergyman who conducts private religious services," originally in great households, later in military regiments, prisons, etc. (http://www.etymonline.com/index.php?term=chaplain)

Chaplains are those who share the love of God
and show compassion wherever there are people in need.

Thus, the chaplaincy refers to the ministry provided by men and women to promote growth and peace for every human being that God sends to them.

The chaplain according to the Encyclopedia Britannica:

A chaplain was originally a priest or minister who took charge of a chapel; it now refers to an ordained member of the clergy who is assigned to a special ministry. The title was used during the first centuries of the Christian church.

Traditionally a chaplain has been a recognized religious servant who is given responsibility for a particular group or institution, usually outside the church, such as hospital chaplains, military chaplains, prison chaplains and school chaplains. How you define 'chaplain' will depend on where that chaplain is serving.

Today, Chaplaincy is a specialized Ministry done by called, anointed, gifted and equipped men and women. They are trained to provide care and support - personally, emotionally, physically, relationally and spiritually. They listen, providing a safe environment for people to share their feelings, and assist people as they work through life's issues. They assist in times of crisis and difficulty. In short, wherever there is a need; there the Chaplain needs to be. Thus, effective chaplains will be someone who is:

- A sensitive and compassionate man or woman who finds meaning ministering to fellow human beings in crisis.
- A professional with the ability to help intervene in crisis and other situations of distress.

The Chaplain is equipped with the ability to:

- Listen
- Provide pastoral care and counseling
- Support
- Advise and give guidance in times of trouble

- A chaplain is responsible and faithful to their faith, respects other faith perspectives, and seeks to support people of all denominations or people without faith.
- A chaplain is a pastor to all, careful not to impose their own values and beliefs on others.
- A chaplain is a person who helps others to reflect and contemplate on:
- The significance of life events
- The source or sources of support available to them (including God of course)

What motivates them towards health and wellness?
Their sense of purpose for now and the future.

- A chaplain works with the fundamental concepts and ideals common to all religions such as: COMMUNITY, TRUST, HOPE, LOVE and RESPONSIBILITY.
- A chaplain is a builder of bridges, emphasizing what we have in common more than our differences (community, family and religion).
- A chaplain has a heart for souls, presenting the gospel in a sensitive manner, praying and ministering with faith and hope, while providing fellowship and other experiences that provide spiritual healing to people.
- A chaplain accepts people where they are and recognizes that many people do not have a theological vocabulary or religious affiliation.
- A chaplain is at home in and is a part of the community in which they serve, whether a medical facility, within prison cells, as hospice workers or other settings, and is able to balance work as a member of the team in the institution in which they serve.
- A chaplain is someone that:
- Grows
- Learns

- Takes risks
- And feels the call of God to be a living epistle for men and women in need of care.

Thus, a chaplain is called, gifted, and able to assist in an institutional setting with all types of people, as a servant to all he or she is privileged to work with, for the glory of God.

4

Hospital Chaplaincy

Important Aspects in the Visitation of Patients

Hospitality and Care of Patients

INTRODUCTION

Like everything else today, I found this excellent introduction on the web.

"A hospital chaplain provides spiritual support in the hospital environment to patients, hospital staff, and family members. In the case of hospitals affiliated with a specific religious denomination, such as Catholic hospitals, the chaplain usually represents the same denomination, while other hospitals can choose chaplains from a variety of backgrounds. Many hospitals stress that although their chaplains belong to specific religious groups, the spiritual services provided are interfaith, meaning that people of all religious faiths will be respected, and that additional religious officiants can be provided upon request.

Chaplains can be found working in a number of environments. They may be fully ordained, as in the case of priests, pastors, and rabbis, or they may simply have received some training. Chaplaincy is often associated specifically with Christianity, but members of other faiths can and do act as chaplains.

In the case of a hospital chaplain, the chaplain works a shift in the hospital, often walking the halls to connect with people who might need spiritual support. He or she provides assistance to members of the staff who may be struggling with religious issues, and religious counseling is also offered to patients and family members. This person may lead religious services in the hospital's chapel or in patient rooms, and services such as Communion may also be offered."

http://www.wisegeek.org/what-does-a-hospital-chaplain-do.htm#didyouknowout

DO's and DON'TS OF PATIENT VISITS

Effective ministry of any kind comes down to preparation and attention…prepare for your visit and pay special attention to the one or ones you are ministering to. The adage know your audience is important here. Thus, we must;

1. Learn to pay attention, not just to words, but the patient's nonverbal language and environment. Open your eyes and ears. Watch out for smells, movements, the look and appearance of the patient. Watch for signs of tension or conflict in their body. Remember, you are ministering to the person, not their room.
2. Evaluate how you project yourself. Do you take time to listen? Do you genuinely feel compassion for the person or are you tempted to judge? Can you communicate with them in a positive, uplifting (as appropriate) manner?
3. Be sensitive, as the patient may be bothered due to their illness and be affected by:
a. odors, perfumes or lack of good hygiene
b. sounds, loud laughter, loud or harsh voice (no speaking in tongues; some people may get a bad impression)
c. personal presentation or quirks - excessive movements, not being very warm; not touching or touching.
4. Listen - Everyone has special spiritual and emotional needs. Learn to identify:
a. anxiety
b. fear (life and death, loss, etc.)
c. guilt (real or pseudo)
d. hostility (what causes it?)
e. loneliness (companionship)
f. insecurity
g. fatigue

h. relaxation
i. bitterness

Get in a comfortable position where the patient sees you in the direction their eyes move. Do not sit on their bed. Be careful when shaking hands or touching the patient. Remember that disease makes them fragile. (Do not visit with plastic gloves or mask, unless told to do so by hospital staff for the benefit of the patient).

5. Learn to control your emotions. Sudden responses of alarm, horror, grief, crying, upset, and so on can be off putting at best. Sometimes patients want to show their surgeries or perhaps due to an accident or surgery their looks have dramatically changed. You need to be emotionally stable and mature as you visit ill individuals.
6. The visit should be short, especially after surgery or an acute illness: 10 to 20 minutes at most.
7. Understand the value of the ministry of presence and companionship. Communicate that "someone cares about him/her," "someone is interested in them," "God remembers him and has not left him." Sometimes all it takes is somebody to be there with the patient, silent and attentive to their needs.
8. Beware of not initiating long or intense conversations. Avoid depressing or disturbing themes. Discuss topics of interest to the patient: family, friends, their past, their future, or what surrounds them (their favorite interests). Be cheerful as you encourage them. (Not all the time will we talk about the Bible; use caution.)
9. The sick like variety, changes, the little surprises, the details. Don't wear or bring anything with fragrance or that can cause allergic reactions; no sweets or fats; one is tempted to indulge.
10. Ask the patient how he has felt since the day before, how he spent the night, or if he's had any visits. Be aware that drugs

can make them sleepy and even slower to speak or think. If they have a concern or complaint regarding their medicine, do not address the question or concern directly, but communicate with the duty nurse or doctor as part of the team.

11. Being heard brings relief, helps them sleep better, increases a sense of hope, frees up energies for recovery and facilitates reconciliation with themselves and others (peace). Do not expect the patient to talk. Sometimes it requires energy that they do not have.
12. Remember that you cannot make any promises of healing. Offer your presence and support to show the compassion and care that God has for us. The person must be willing and open to receive God's grace in their suffering. In fact, you, the sick person, medical personnel and family members all depend on God's grace. If the person you are ministering to is a believer and asks for prayer (you can also ask), pray for healing and comfort, blessing and strength, as you sense the leading of the Holy Spirit…but again, be sensitive to the setting and always the needs of the patient you serve.
13. If the patient is in the process of recovery, help them to imagine that within a reasonable time period the present situation will be a memory (do not give any dates).
14. If the patient asks you, "Do you think I'm going to get well?" and you are unsure: Do not lie – ask them "What has the doctor told you?" "That's our hope." "We're all wishing that you recover soon and are praying for you towards that end."
15. Do not speak softly or whisper in front of the patient where he can see or hear. Your conversation may be innocent but may leave doubts and fears in the patient. When you say goodbye, mean it and don't linger on.
16. Reach out to the family and ask how they're coping in the middle of their family member's illness. Be aware of their needs and reactions.

17. Remember that stress plays an important role in pain and pain management. The pain is real to the patient, whether it is of an organic nature or psychological. Listen - this relieves the tension. Do not make promises of help or support you may not be able to keep.

GENERAL GUIDELINES

1. Do not be offended by the patient who may reject your visit or responds to your care in a negative way. You must not be easily offended. Do not be antagonistic. Pain can affect their mood and give the appearance of ungratefulness. Do not argue with the family or judge how they are coping with the illness of their family member, as everyone deals with crisis differently. Always assume that the patient is a good person, doing the best they can in difficult circumstances.
2. Prepare ahead of time when visiting a patient. Leave behind your personal stresses and agenda. You must be able to concentrate to hear the unique concerns of each patient. Leave your worries and problems behind in preparation for the visit.

The focus should be on the:

1. The needs of the person you are visiting.
2. Our relationship with them.
3. Sharing of our presence as a testimony of the love of Jesus Christ.
4. Ministry, to include praying before visiting to clear your mind and give you strength.
5. Remember that in the face of affliction there is no favorite patient. All individuals are the focus of God's love and mercy.
6. Do not argue: listen. Arguments stress the mind that needs rest. When arguing with the patient, you are closing doors to healing communication.

7. Do not repeat stories or gossip about the patient. You may listen to confidential information. (Learn the value of loyalty and mercy. Do not talk about the disease to others).

RIGHTS OF PATIENTS

Most medical facilities are bound by and disseminate guidelines regarding the rights of patients. These are the most relevant items on the Letter of General Rights of Patients:

1. Receive adequate medical care. The medical assistant should be trained in accordance with the needs of their health and circumstances that provide this support must inform you in advance should you require the attention of another specialist
2. Receive dignity and respect. Regardless the social or economic situation of the patient, dignity and respect must be shown at all times to the patient and their family.
3. Receive sufficient, clear, timely and professional care. The physician has an obligation to inform the patient or the person responsible in a clear and understandable way, the diagnosis, prognosis and treatment plan, which allows the patient or family to make necessary health related decisions.
4. Freely decide about their care. The patient or supervisor can accept or reject without pressure, any type of treatment, or the use of extraordinary measures of survival when suffering a terminal illness.
5. Be granted informed consent. The patient, or legal guardian, must be informed of the risks involving any and all medical procedures, in writing, thus allowing the patient opportunity to agree to or refuse said treatment. This includes experimental research and organ donation.
6. Be treated with confidentiality. Under no circumstances should physicians or other allied health professionals (including Chaplains) disseminate information that will violate the trust of their patients. In most cases, written

authorization for sharing information must be given, including personal information derived from research studies to which the patient has volunteered for, except when compelled by law.
7. Have the ability to get a second opinion. The patient should receive written information about diagnosis, prognosis or treatment related to your health to get a second opinion from another specialist, if desired.
8. Medical care in case of emergency. Without exception, whenever an accident or illness is life-threatening, health institutions, public or private are required to provide emergency medical care in order to stabilize their conditions.
9. Having a medical record. If needed, they must give a written summary that is accurate, clear, and in an understandable form, which fully summarizes the care received.
10. Be addressed even if it is dissatisfied by the care received. Medical authorities of the institution, whether public or private have an obligation to listen and respond to a patient complaint, especially if they are not satisfied that the medical service provided was done in a professional manner.

HOSPITALITY AND CARE OF PATIENTS

The Objective

- To equip the volunteer chaplain with the concepts and principles of the hospitality of patient care.
- To implement the practical aspects of patient care with professional interpersonal skills.

THE PRINCIPLES OF HOSPITALITY PATIENTS

Hospitality Care Principles serve as the basis for professionals to be effective in the industry of health care. The Principles are:

- Genuine Care
- The Purpose of Your Call
- The Ability to Respond
- Identifying and supporting the Mission of the Organization / Institution
- Identifying your personal contribution to the Organization
- The Continuity of Patient Care

Each principle is correlated to the other. If we separate the principles from each other, we weaken there meaning and purpose.

Webster defines hospitality as:

- The friendly reception and treatment of guests or strangers, an act or statement of welcome. The quality of being hospitable; welcoming guests or strangers. As chaplains, being hospitable, kind, and caring are to be characteristics of our ministry.
- What is genuine care?
- Along with hospitality, we need to be willing to provide genuine care, which is defined as the sincere and total devotion to quality service, while doing all we can to accommodate each patient and his family. Genuine care is appealing to all who enter an institution, a dispensary, a room or an executive office. Genuine care helps to facilitate a positive environment that makes those who need help and direction feel welcome and valued.

How can we exemplify genuine care?

- Genuine care is seen as we practice the seven personal skills that every health professional, hospital chaplain and paraprofessional should learn. The development of these skills is paramount to the success of quality hospitality for patients. They are:
- Warm genuineness, or the ability to communicate to an individual with respect.

- Observation, which is the ability to sense the environment and situations one is dealing with in the present.
- Encouraging people in need by asking questions within your ability and knowledge of their situation.
- Active listening is the ability to effectively demonstrate receptivity to their needs and concerns.
- Every patient in your care requires information directly and respectfully as you answer questions.
- Along with answering questions, chaplains need to respond with action as soon as possible to a reasonable and necessary request.
- Overall, and most importantly, the chaplain must have strong communication skills which includes the ability to exchange information between two or more people. Also, it often takes patience and perseverance to communicate effectively with people in your care.

Genuine care is something that every chaplain, and other allied health care provider strives to give, as it demonstrates a major aspect of our purpose and calling.

What is the Purpose of Your Calling?

The purpose of your calling reveals the major factor that motivates and fills your life with meaning or importance, and what God has destined for us as his sons and daughters. The purpose of your call is determined by three factors:

- The need to serve, which should be part of the calling and purpose of every believer. For the chaplain, our need to serve is focused on the clients we minister to, in the setting God has provided for us.
- The need for leadership, that is, to make a difference in others' lives through our service to others. We are to lead by example, with true servant leadership, as demonstrated in the life and ministry of Jesus.

- The desire to positively impact lives through our service. Much of the impact we make will be unheralded, unnoticed, and unacknowledged, by people, but never by the Lord. Thus, in our calling, as we fulfill our purpose, we must have:

The Ability to Respond

The ability to respond begins with submission to authority. As a Chaplain, we are committed and submitted to God, and we are submitted to the governmental regulations of the organization in which we serve. The way we respond to authority and delegate authority demonstrates the maturity and integrity of our lives and calling.

1. How do you respond? We must, always be seasoned with grace and humility. This requires that we have a clear perception of the chain of command. It does not matter know someone became a boss or superior, we are to show them respect due their office or position.
2. What is your perception as a follower? The fact is, we are not responsible for how others treat us, but we are responsible to respond responsibly to colleagues' criticism, whether warranted or not. It is essential that we believe and practice personal responsibility.

It is essential that we, as servants of God and the institution in which we work, be responsible and accountable in our response to the people we serve.

Identify the Mission of the Institution/Organization

Many established organizations in the United States promote their beliefs and causes through a mission statement. The history and progress of the organization are evidence of their mission.

A mission is the pursuit of a specific service or calling for the improvement of others or of oneself.

As a chaplain, it is important to know the mission of the organization in which you serve. Along with knowing the mission, and understanding your role in the organization, it is helpful to fully comprehend the policies of the organization and be able to serve in the organization according to the mission and values of the organization, and thus be able to make a strong contribution to its mission.

Again, it should go without saying, but we say it anyway, you need to know the organization you serve at, as you represent both the Lord and the organization you are attached to especially, know the mission of the organization.

Identify Your Outstanding Contribution To The Organization

Along with knowing the mission, it is essential that one identify and articulate what contribution you make to the organization you serve. You must ask yourself the question, "Is my contribution noticed and celebrated, or merely tolerated?" In other words, does your contribution "fit" within the institution?

All of us want to make a difference. If we are not celebrated, perhaps we are not in the right position or the right setting.

The Continuity of Patient Care Hospitality:

Continuity of patient care, which includes hospitality, is preserved by the vigilance that is given by those who require welfare but lack understanding of the world of healthcare. The greatest service we can offer, beyond the ministry of presence, is to assist those who are powerless to help themselves.

5

Chaplaincy in the Justice System

History and Function

"For the LORD is our Judge, the LORD is our Lawgiver, the LORD is our King; He will save us."

Isaiah 33:2

INTRODUCTION

God seeks justice for everyone. The Bible, particularly the OT Laws provide a model for the fair and just treatment of individuals. When serving in prison ministry as a chaplain, there is much to know…and it starts with God's perspective on all people, including those incarcerated.

The True Fast—Isaiah 58:6-10

Is not this the fast that I have chosen? To loose the bands of wickedness, to undo the heavy burdens, and to let the oppressed go free, and that you break every yoke? Is it not to deal thy bread to the hungry, and that thou bring the poor that are cast out to thy house? when you see the naked, that you cover him; and that you hide not thyself from your own flesh?

Then shall your light break forth as the morning, and your health shall spring forth speedily: and thy righteousness shall go before you; the glory of the LORD shall be your reward.

Then shall you call, and the LORD shall answer; you shall cry, and he shall say, Here I am. If you take away from the midst of thee the yoke, the putting forth of the finger, and speaking vanity; And if you draw out your soul to the hungry, and satisfy the afflicted soul; then shall your light rise in obscurity, and thy darkness be as the noonday: And the LORD shall guide you continually, and satisfy your soul in drought, and make fat your bones: and you shall be like a watered garden, and like a spring of water, whose waters never fail. And they that shall be of you shall build the old waste places: you shall raise up the foundations of many generations; and you shall be called, The repairer of the breach, The restorer of paths to dwell in.

Of course, there are many other scriptures that speak of the importance of justice and mercy which include:

> *"Do not take advantage of a widow or an orphan. If you do and they cry out for me, I will certainly hear their cry."*
>
> Exodus 22:22-23

> *"Do not deny justice to the poor people in their lawsuits. Have nothing to do with a false charge and do not put an innocent or honest person to death for I will not acquit the guilty."*
>
> Exodus 23:6-7

> *"Do not oppress an alien, you yourselves know how it feels to be aliens, because you were aliens in Egypt."*
>
> Exodus 23:9

Thus, we should strive to see justice and mercy in:

Social laws –which includes injuries, homicide, destroyed property, etc. (Exodus 20 to 23)

Moral laws – sexual immorality, honesty, thievery, idolatry. (Leviticus 18 to 20)

Governmental leadership – leadership & righteousness. (Leviticus. 16 to 21)

History Of The American Justice System

We have come a long way, and no doubt more changes are needed to ensure that we have a fair and just justice system. We may not be where we should be, but thankfully we are not as we once were.

The conditions of the justice system of the 18th century were harsh and cruel, even by the standards of the day. Execution was the punishment for most crimes, including theft. Poor houses and prisons housed paupers and debtors.

The practice of torture and secret trials was also common among the judicial system of the day. Torture was used to extract a confession or information from a suspect. Punishment included mutilation, excess (cutting the tongue or hand), whipping, branding, etc.

The philosophers and writers of the "Enlightenment" contributed to the reformation of the judicial system by advocating the banning of torture and insisting on punishments that fit the crime.

"The Enlightenment" drastically changed the way the Western world thought about justice. Enlightenment thinkers established many of the democratic principles that formed the conceptual foundations of the American and French revolutions.

THE COURTS AND THE PROCESS

Though there are unique aspects of the U.S. judicial system (such as innocent until proven guilty), the foundation of the American justice system is the English Common Law and our court is patterned after the English Court system. Most Western modern judicial systems derive from the same root.

The Arrest Process

One of the foundational principles of a Western judicial system is related to the concept of due process. Due process is defined as "a fundamental, constitutional guarantee that all legal proceedings will be fair and that one will be given notice of the proceedings and an opportunity to be heard before the government acts to take away one's life, liberty, or property." (The Free Dictionary) The Fourteenth Amendment to the Constitution promises "Due Process."

...nor shall any State deprive any person of life, liberty, or property, without due process of law; nor deny to any person within its jurisdiction the equal protection of the laws.

This Constitutional guarantee is granted to all citizens of the United States, and most if not all visitors to the United States as well, whether legal or alien. Thus, as a chaplain, the rights of the prisoner are important, as are the rights of victims. More on this will be provided below, but first a review of the various courts.

The Various Courts

There are many different courts, which adjudicate different types of problems or offenses. A basic knowledge of the court system can help the prison chaplain to relate to the process an offender may have travailed through and the types of issues the prisoner may have to deal with while incarcerated, or after release.

THE CRIMINAL COURT

The Criminal Court has jurisdiction over misdemeanors and felonies. Judges of the Criminal Court also act as arraigning magistrates and conduct preliminary hearings in felony cases.

THE SUPREME COURT

The trial court of unlimited original jurisdiction, but it generally only hears cases that are outside the jurisdiction of other trial courts of more limited jurisdiction. It exercises civil jurisdiction and jurisdiction over felony charges.

THE FAMILY COURT

The Family Court hears matters involving children and families.

Its jurisdiction includes: custody and visitation, support, family offense (domestic violence), persons in need of supervision, delinquency, child protective proceedings (abuse and neglect), foster care approval and review, termination of parental rights, adoption and guardianship.

CIVIL COURT

The Civil Court has jurisdiction over civil cases involving amounts up to $25,000 and other civil matters referred to it by the Supreme Court.

It includes a small claims division for informal disposition of matters not exceeding a certain dollar amount designated by each state, and a housing part for landlord-tenant matters and housing code violations.

THE SURROGATE'S COURT

The Surrogate's Court hears cases involving the affairs of decedents, including the probate of wills and the administration of estates, and adoptions.

THE JUVENILE COURT

The juvenile court oversees matters related to minors.

PRISON STATISTICS FROM THE DEPARTMENT OF JUSTICE OF THE UNITED STATES

Prison statistics vary from nation to nation. Within most Western cultures, there is at least an openness to statistics, as in many non-Western nations. It is virtually anyone's guess how many men and women are incarcerated, for what crimes, and for what duration. Here are some up to date statistics on prisons in the United States. If you are in a nation that is open, you can usually find similar statistics through government websites.

- As of December 31, 2001, there were an estimated 5.6 million adults who had served in the state or federal prison,

including 4.3 million former prisoners and 1.3 million convicts in prison.
- Almost a third of former prisoners were still under correctional supervision, including 731,000 on probation, 437,000 on parole, and 166,000 in local jails.
- Women formed 6.6% of inmates in the prisons of the United States in 2001, compared with 6% in 1995.
- 64% of prison inmates belonged to racial or ethnic minorities in 2001. Sadly, this statistic remains mostly unchanged.

Among the prisoners in the state prison system:

- Almost half were sentenced for a violent crime (49%) - One-fifth were sentenced for a crime against property (20%).
- Nearly a fifth were sentenced for drug-related crimes (21%).
- 48% of women prisoners had reported being physically or sexually abused prior to admission, 27% of them had been raped.
- From the 272,111 people released from prisons in 15 states in 1994, 67.5% were rearrested for a felony within 3 years, 46.9% were convicted again, 25.4% were sentenced for a different crime. Sadly, the recidivism rate amongst the prison population remains high…the need for faith-based solution to this problem is only increasing.
- In a day in the year 1994 there were approximately 234,000 offenders convicted of rape or sexual assault under the care, custody, or control of correctional agencies, almost 60% of these sex offenders are under conditional supervision in the community.
- 4 out of 10 prisoners spent some time in jail for domestic violence and had acted out while on probation or under a restraining order.
- Among the 5.3 million convicted offenders under the jurisdiction of correctional agencies in 1996, it was estimated that almost 2 million, or about 36%, were drinking

alcohol at the time of the crime. Treatment of substance abusers, in the prison and upon release is another major area of need that can be addressed by well trained and positioned chaplains.
- In 1998 there were an estimated 3.2 million women arrested, 22% of all arrests that year.

These are just a few of the statistics regarding incarceration in the United States many more could be obtained for various websites, such as the Bureau of Justice Statistics. https://bjs.gov/

The purpose for this review is to simply sensitize the reader to the great need for chaplains to consider the needs of the incarcerated as well as their victims and families of both. There is perhaps no great opportunity for true ministry as can be found in a prison or similar setting. This need is second to the recovery ministry at large. The more we know about the justice system and those involved the more effective we can be as caregivers and servants of Christ.

6

The Chaplain in Prisons

INTRODUCTION

The role of a chaplain is to provide and convey an attitude of love, understanding and concern toward inmates. The Chaplain represents the religious community and official authority. The chaplain helps prisoners to prepare themselves to successfully integrate back into the community once they are released. This support ministry begins in the institution where the inmate establishes a relationship with the church community through the chaplain. In other words, the chaplain is a connection between the inmate's reform and the community. Thus, as a chaplain, it is imperative to see the prisoner as:

- A person created in the image of God with dignity and the ability to receive God's mercy and forgiveness through faith.
- An individual able to become a new creature in Jesus Christ, and to grow and mature in faith, demonstrated by a truly changed life (you must believe change is possible for all).

A unique individual, loved by God, and deserving of value and respect.

As a prison chaplain, one must assume several roles. Sometimes she/he is:

- A friend
- An assistant
- A counselor
- A constructive critic. Thus, the chaplain should be:
- Mature and flexible (blessed are the flexible, for they shall not be broken)
- With both feet firmly on the ground and our head in the clouds enough to hear from heaven for others

- Must have great faith in God, his grace, mercy, kindness and power to bring change and not seek personal gratification.

"To a chaplain, serving is his reward"

HISTORY AND TRADITION

In the days of corporal punishment, it was the clerics who brought humane treatment into the penal institutions. They brought relief, hope and strength to the inmate's faith. This remains an integral part of Christian doctrine, which requires us to not forget the incarcerated but rather to visit them. (See Isaiah 42:7; 58:6-7 and 61:1 and Matt. 25) Clerics were the first educators, counselors and social workers in the penal system. This responsibility has been transferred to the chaplains.

MINISTERING TO PRISONERS

There are several important things to consider as you begin ministering in a prison setting. First and foremost, you must obey all regulations of the institution that you visit, as well as the ministry you represent.

First Part: The Preparation

Ministering in correctional ministry is very intense. You should be prepared to deal with natural and spiritual forces.

One must prepare in a number of ways, which include prayer, intercession or what is often called spiritual warfare. For certain, there are forces of evil that fight against an inmates' conversion, growth and success. A chaplain must be a person of genuine prayer, though it need not always be formal, but more an attitude of awareness of God's presence and the acknowledgement of his goodness and ability to bring about good for all involved.

Secondly, chaplains must be men and women of the Word: One must understand and be able to use scripture appropriately. Knowing the Word is important, but the proper utilization of scripture is key. One help in this regard is the book "The Bible in Counseling" by

Dr. Stan DeKoven more information on this book is found under "additional resources" in the back of this book.

Along with spiritual preparation we need natural, common sense preparation as well. Thus, we must do our homework before ministry. We cannot successfully simply walk into a jail or Prison certain steps must be taken. We must:

- Find out the regulations and make an appointment to visit.
- Meet with others who are already working in the prison or jail and learn the ways of operation.
- Be willing to follow a leader until you are ready to take leadership yourself.
- Plan how to dress and what to take with you as you begin your journey. In light of these simple, common sense steps, here are some the key things to be aware of before entering into a prison setting for ministry.

ENTERING THE PRISON: DO'S AND DON'TS

Many of these items may seem self-explanatory or even trite…but they are important. Remember, you are an invited guest into a very different world…you have much to learn. These principles and recommendations are in no certain order; all are designed to help you have a good experience when you start ministry, and help you avoid various potential pitfalls.

1. When visiting a prison, your vehicle must have all their legal papers in order; insurance up to date and the driver must have a valid driver's license.
2. A correctional officer will inspect the vehicle in what is referred to as the "Sally Port."

If all is in order, you will pass through the gate with ease. Once inside:

1. A Correctional Officer will stop you at the front door.

2. Make sure you DO NOT BRING CELL PHONES, BEEPERS or recorders. Leave these items in the vehicle.
3. Obviously, No weapons - guns, knives or smuggling (i.e. nail clippers, Swiss Army knife, cigarettes, etc.) is permitted…and if you try such things, you might be invited for a longer stay!
4. Do not lend or give prisoners pens, pencils, and instruments with metal or sharp points.
5. You should not bring with you any food, candy, gum. Your role is not to be friends with inmates; friendly yes, but your currency of exchange is your gift of ministry.
6. All personal belongings and bags will be scanned by an X-ray machine, as with airport screenings.
7. All visitors must have a photo ID to be allowed to enter.
8. You must wear a visitor's pass and it needs to be visible at all times.
9. Do not bring literature except a Bible or tracks.
10. Do not bring hard cover Bibles. Avoid any spiral bound literature and paper clips. These can become weapons and will likely be confiscated.
11. Review all the Bible tracks and the biblical literature with the ministry leader. If possible, read all tracks before they are delivered to prisoners and make sure the content is purely religious, not political or offensive.

NOTE: If you lose your visitor's pass, you will be retained and treated as a prisoner until the pass is recovered and the Supervisor of the Security Office determines that you are indeed a visitor. Entering a secure facility, such as a prison, is not for the faint of heart and is serious business. We must treat it as such.

PROPER ATTIRE

- Though you are entering a correctional institution, where prisoners do not dress for success, you should

dress appropriately. Sneakers, sandals, and some other clothes are not allowed.
- Men and women should wear clothes that do not have multiple parts (i.e. jackets, sweaters). If you have to remove clothing and place them on a chair or table, they can be taken.
- Women must not wear tight clothing that might accentuate the curves of their body. The purpose is for prisoners to focus on the Word of God not on you.
- Leave jewelry at home, expensive watches or earrings can be stolen or used for dangerous purposes.

BEING GUIDED IN JAIL

- Once everyone in a Ministry Team has met the procedures at the front door, a Correction Officer will be assigned to accompany the Ministry Team to the designated area where "the Service" will take place.
- Follow the guidelines provided by the Correctional Officer.
- Do not wander around the halls. As you walk through the halls, inmates will also be accompanied by Correctional Officers.
- Do not talk to the prisoners or respond to their comments while walking the halls.
- If you find a corrections officer who accompanies a prisoner in chains, shackles or handcuffs, do not stop to talk or try to give a track or pray with them. Do not ask questions or make comments.
- If there is some disturbance such as a fire, a fight, and so on, do not leave the area assigned to you, and follow the instructions of the corrections officers.

ONCE APPOINTED TO THE SERVICE AREA

- Stay in the area assigned to you until you are escorted outside or given other directions if there is an emergency.
- Follow the correctional officer's instructions. He or she is your security as you lead the service.
- If a need arises while leading the service, the ministry Leader will ask the Correctional Officer for assistance. This is to avoid confusion.
- The ministry Leader should start the service, lead the inmates and introduce the ministry team, if necessary.
- The beginning and the ending of the service must be completed on schedule. Remember that time is short; focus on the purpose of your visit.
- Choose songs that prisoners can sing and participate in during the service.
- Do not use last names, only the first name, using the term Brother or Sister.
- Do not give your phone number or home address. Give the number of the ministry as appropriate and approved by the ministry leader.
- All correspondence should be addressed to the ministry.
- Do not accept any correspondence from an inmate to be given to a family member or friend. All mail should be addressed to the prison ministry.
- Do not give any correspondence or any items to the inmates.
- Do not promise anyone that you will help with a bond, surety or guarantor. Remember, you are chaplain, representing the Lord and the ministry through which you serve. You are not a lawyer, a psychologist or social worker…remember your role and place.

AFTER THE SERVICE ENDS

- The prisoners will approach team members, to thank and greet them. Sometimes they will ask for contact information.
- Be very discreet in what you share with an inmate, as mentioned above.
- Women should be fully aware that for some prisoners' worship is a time for recreation. Do not get into long conversations. The prisoners can be very manipulative in this regard and have ulterior motives for spending time with a female...enough said.
- If asked when the ministry team will return, direct them to the ministry leader who is in charge of planning. The last thing you want to do is give inmates wrong information; they lose trust easily.

In Isaiah 61, Luke 4, the word specifically mentions visiting prisoners thus, it is a great ministry to help men and women in prison it is a true expression of the heart of God.

7

Theology of Prison Ministry

"You Came Unto Me..."

The Biblical Mandate for Ministry to a prisoner is best stated in the gospel of Matthew.

> *I was in prison, and you came to me.*
>
> Matthew 25:36

The Lord himself was (temporarily) a prisoner, one who was left to the harshest of punishments. He was, of course, innocent of any crime, but punished as a criminal. No doubt the Lord recognizes the special sense of isolation that perhaps only a prisoner might feel and knew that the thing most needed is a visit from one who cares.

INTRODUCTION

Barbed wire, steel bars and heavy metal doors. Guard towers with armed officers and criminals. This is prison!

- Society says, "Lock them up and throw away the key."
- Politicians say, "We need to build more prisons."
- Statistics say, "80% of inmates return to prison after release--we are wasting our time to try to rehabilitate them."

But Jesus says, "I was in prison, and you came to me."

The prison system is the only "business" that succeeds by its failure. Prison populations grow larger and larger. Often, people come out of prison worse than when they went in. Many commit more crimes, return to prison, and get stuck in the cycle of recidivism, the "revolving door" of crime, prison, and release.

The answer to this is not more prisons. It is not locking people up and "throwing away the key." It is not even the death penalty, as studies have shown that even this does not effectively deter crime.

The answer is the Gospel of Jesus Christ in the demonstration of power!

Prisoners need regeneration not rehabilitation--and Jesus has commissioned His followers to reach beyond the barbed wire fences and steel bars to touch the lives of men and women bound by the shackles of sin.

THE MANDATE FOR PRISON MINISTRY

The mandate for prison ministry is clear in God's Word, both by scripture and example.

The greatest scriptural mandate for prison ministry is given in Matthew 25:31-40. Jesus said:

> *"When the Son of Man comes in His glory, and all the holy angels with Him, then He will sit on the throne of His glory. All the nations will be gathered before Him, and He will separate them one from another, as a shepherd divides his sheep from the goats. And He will set the sheep on His right hand, but the goats on the left. Then the King will say to those on His right hand, `Come, you blessed of My Father, inherit the kingdom prepared for you from the foundation of the world: `for I was hungry and you gave Me food; I was thirsty and you gave Me drink; I was a stranger and you took Me in; `I was naked and you clothed Me; I was sick and you visited Me; I was in prison and you came to Me.' Then the righteous will answer Him, saying, `Lord, when did we see You hungry and feed You, or thirsty and give You drink? When did we see You a stranger and take You in, or naked and clothe You? Or when did we see You sick, or in prison, and come to You?' And the King will answer and say to them, `Assuredly, I say to you, in as much as you did it to one of the least of these My brethren, you did it to Me.'"*
>
> Matthew 25:31-40

EXAMPLE

Jesus Christ Himself is our example for prison ministry. One of the main targets of Christ's Ministry was prisoners:

> *"To open blind eyes, to bring out the prisoners from the prison, and them that sit in darkness out of the prison house."*
>
> Isaiah 42:7

Jesus declared:

> *"The spirit of the Lord God is upon me; because the Lord hath anointed me to preach good tidings unto the meek; he hath sent me to bind up the brokenhearted, to proclaim liberty to the captives, and the opening of the prison to them that are bound"*
>
> Isaiah 61:1

Even while dying on Calvary's cross, Jesus took time to reach out in love and concern to a prisoner. As a result, that convicted criminal experienced God's love, grace, and forgiveness. During the time between His death and resurrection, we are told that Jesus "went and preached to the spirits in prison" (1 Peter 3:19).

Unfortunately, despite the clear Biblical injunction and Christ's example to minister to prisoners, many believers prefer to pass by on the other side of the street, as did the religious leaders in the parable of the Good Samaritan (see Luke 10:29-37).

WHY PRISON MINISTRY?

Why must believers be concerned about prison ministry?

1. Prison ministry has a direct Scriptural mandate (Matthew 25:31-40). Throughout the Bible are examples, descriptions, and commandments about prisons, prisoners, bondage,

captivity, and slavery. The Bible mentions prison, prisoners, or imprisonment more than 130 times.
2. We should follow the example Christ set by ministering to prisoners.
3. Prisons meet the criteria of any mission field: Lost people and a need for laborers.
4. God is not willing that any should perish--not even serial killers, rapists, and molesters (2 Peter 3:9). God loves even the "worst of sinners" (1 Timothy 1:15).
5. Professional (paid) Chaplains cannot minister to more than a small percentage of inmates in their care. They cannot do all of the necessary work themselves, as there is just not enough time to do so.
6. Many jails and prisons have no professional chaplains, and many have no religious services at all.
7. For every person incarcerated, there are three to five other people affected: Mates, children, parents, etc. Inmates and their families represent a large segment of society in any culture.
8. False religions and cults are reaching out to prisoners. We must get there first with the Gospel of Jesus Christ!

GOALS OF PRISON MINISTRY

The spiritual goals of jail and prison ministry may include one, some, or all of the following:

- To share the unconditional love of God.
- To present the Gospel of Jesus Christ in such a way that inmates will embrace it and receive Christ as Savior.
- To disciple new believers in the Word and teach them how to study the Bible.
- To demonstrate the power of prayer and teach them to pray.

- To lead inmates to experience the life-changing power of God that will free them from guilt, shame, negative emotions, and addictions.
- To minister to inmates' families.
- The social goals of jail and prison ministry are:
- To help the inmate function more positively within the prison environment.
- To provide a link between the community and persons confined in correctional institutions.
- To prepare residents for re-entry into society (physically, mentally, morally and spiritually).
- To assist inmates' families in practical ways.
- To provide post-prison assistance in practical ways.

WHAT THE GOSPEL HAS TO OFFER

The Gospel of Jesus Christ has many things to offer inmates.

- Forgiveness from sin.
- A chance to say, "I'm sorry."
- Release from guilt and shame.
- Acceptance -- all many of them have ever known is rejection.
- New values and perspectives.
- Strategies for coping with difficult situations and negative emotions.
- Basics for true, honest relationships.
- Life abundant through Jesus Christ.
- A new purpose for living.
- Eternal life.

WHAT IS YOUR ROLE?

Of the millions of active believers world-wide, only a small number are involved in ministry to prisoners, even though jails and prisons are found in almost every community. Yet the scriptural mandate by both teaching and example is clear.

Every believer should be involved in prison ministry. This does not necessarily mean you are called to go into a prison. As in foreign missions--not everyone is called to go to a foreign field to share the Gospel. But--as in missions--every believer should be involved in prison ministry in some capacity.

There are many ways to be involved. Here are but a few:

- Provide prayer support for prison ministries.
- Visit an inmate.
- Write to a prisoner.
- Assist families of inmates.
- Help inmates transition back to society after their release.
- Conduct worship services, Bible studies, or group meetings inside prisons.
- Write, publish, and distribute Biblically based training material specifically designed for prison inmates.
- Provide Bibles and Christian literature for inmates.
- Provide financial support to a prison ministry.
- Serve as a prison chaplain…which we hope you are seriously considering as you read this book and take this Vision International University course.

Begin now to pray for God to reveal the specific way that you are to be involved!

Qualifications and Preparation

KEY VERSE

Be an example to the believers in word, in conduct, in love, in spirit.

Titus 2:7-8

INTRODUCTION

Those who minister with inmates must be sure of their relationship with Christ, set a proper example, and always be ready to give an answer for the hope within them. While a person called to this ministry should demonstrate all the spiritual virtues taught in the Word, this chapter emphasizes the essential qualifications prison workers should possess.

SPIRITUAL QUALIFICATIONS

COURAGE

Entering a jail or prison to minister--whether on a one-to-one or group basis--is outside the "comfort zone" for most believers. It is not unusual to feel a bit uneasy the first few times you are in a penal facility---but remember, God will take care of you whenever you are in His service. In most cases, the prison chapel is a safe place and inmates are open and friendly. If you feel apprehensive, remember that God does not give a spirit of fear--so recognize where fear comes from and conquer it in the name of Jesus!

COOPERATION

There are many different persons functioning in many different roles in prison society. As a volunteer-in addition to the inmates-you will primarily be involved with correctional officers (also called guards) and a chaplain or supervisor. Most people you meet will probably treat you with courtesy and respect. Be sure to treat them courteously, speaking to them and shaking hands with them where appropriate, using their names when reasonably possible. A good prison worker knows how to cooperate with others--administration, other volunteers, and especially the chaplain, if the jail or prison has one.

It is important for you, as a volunteer, to have some understanding of the work of jail and prison chaplains. Chaplains work long hours under difficult conditions. Each day chaplains must deal with many responsibilities such as the personal crises of inmates, providing programs to meet the spiritual needs of inmates, and fighting the frustrations and disappointments which are an integral part of prison chaplaincy.

Most full-time prison and jail chaplains have more training and preparation for their work than do many ministers. Before they can be accepted into many prisons, they must have seminary training and be endorsed by their denominations. Often, they are required to have served in a pastorate before coming into chaplaincy. Chaplains must also be acceptable to the warden of the prison in which he/she is to work.

A chaplain functions as the administrator of a religious program for the entire institution. He/she provides for the traditional preaching and worship functions, oversees religious education programs; spends much time in personal counseling; recruits, trains and supervises volunteers; and performs many administrative activities (letters, meetings, reports.)

It is important for volunteers to maintain a good relationship with the institutional chaplain. It is a grave breach of trust to use your access to the prison to undermine the chaplain's reputation or to discredit his programs. If there is a problem, always talk with the chaplain first.

GENUINENESS

Be real! Inmates are adept at identifying phonies. A person should not visit the prison with an improper motive like seeking a spouse of showing off his/her abilities. Prisoners are extremely perceptive. They can quickly spot the person who joined the team out of curiosity. Selfish motives and "holier-than-thou" attitudes have no place in this ministry.

HUMILITY

Maintain a humble spirit. Remember--you are there to serve. Always be in subjection to those in authority (the chaplain, guards, warden).

FORGIVING

Foster a forgiving spirit, recognizing that but for the grace of God; you could be in a similar situation. Realize that God's forgiveness extends to what society calls "psychopaths" and the "vilest of individuals."

PERSEVERANCE

Society, friends, and family have given up on many inmates. They don't need someone else to reject them. Be patient. God has promised you will reap spiritual fruit in due season. Volunteers who start and then quit demoralize the inmate, disappoint the chaplain and the prison staff, and present a bad image to the efforts of the church.

FAITHFULNESS

Be faithful, consistent, and trustworthy in the performance of your duties, especially in keeping promises and being on time for appointments or services. The prison chaplain depends on you, as do the inmates. A visit that may just be another in a long list of things you have to do can be the highlight of an inmate's week. Don't disappoint them. Be faithful to this great privilege with which God has entrusted you. Commitment to be consistent and dependable is a quality valued by chaplains who work with volunteers.

EMPATHY

Empathy is the ability to feel with people as though you were in their place. In the Old Testament, the Prophet Ezekiel sat with the captives by the River Chebar before he shared God's message to them. They were ready to listen, because they knew he understood. He had "sat where they sat" (Ezekiel 1:1). What inmates do not need is sympathy…to feel sorry for them. An attitude of sympathy denigrates the worth of a man or woman. Do not play into self-pity. Empathy empowers someone to see themselves as God does; created in his image and likeness for a purpose.

SENSE OF MISSION

A sense of mission is a desire and determination to give this work priority (at the times designated for it), a belief that this is what you would rather be doing (at that time) than anything else in the world!

SPIRITUAL GROWTH

You must not only lead inmates to new spiritual growth, but likewise you must be willing and anxious to grow. Spiritual growth is a lifelong process. If you ever feel that you have "arrived" in either knowledge or virtue, you are simply showing how immature you really are.

EMOTIONAL MATURITY

It is important that you can handle your own emotions: Anger, depression, up one day and down the next. Prison is a depressing place and inmates don't need more gloom and doom.

LOVE

Study 1 Corinthians 13. The greatest motivating force behind any ministry--and especially prison ministry--is love. Love for God, love for the inmate, love for the mission to which God has called you.

PREPARATION

There are four vital areas of preparation for those who desire to be effective prison ministers.

1. PREPARE IN PRAYER

As previously stated, but needing to be emphasized, effective prison ministry is fueled by prayer. Here are some specific prayer targets:

- The chaplain of the institution.
- Individual inmates.
- Families of inmates.
- The warden and administrative staff.
- Correction officers.
- Safety for prison volunteers entering the institution.

- Parolees: For their spiritual and practical needs--jobs, housing.
- Revelation knowledge to meet the needs of inmates.
- For God to raise up strong spiritual leaders within the prison church body.
- Inmate prayer requests: Many prison chapels have a prayer request box. Inmates write out their requests and put them in the box for the chaplain and volunteers to pray specifically for their concerns.

2. PREPARE IN THE WORD

The prison volunteer should have a good working knowledge of the Bible and basic Christianity. Most inmates are not interested in the finer points of theology, but they do need a clear, understandable presentation of the gospel. If you do not study and understand the Word, how can you help someone else learn to study and understand it? To be an effective prison worker, you must continually be studying God's Word.

3. PREPARE FOR YOUR SPECIFIC RESPONSIBILITY

Prepare for your specific responsibility in ministry. If you are to sing, have your sound track cued and ready. If you are to teach, spend adequate time preparing your lesson. If you are using video or audio equipment, have these items ready.

4. PREPARE FOR THE SPECIFIC INSTITUTION

Prepare yourself for the specific institutional setting you will enter:

- Know the rules for dress and conduct of the specific institution. These vary from institution to institution.
- Know the chain of command, to whom you are responsible as a volunteer.
- Know what you can take into the institution with you.

- Get a general understanding of the ways in which acceptable Christian ministries can be carried out within that system.
- Attend training and orientation classes offered by the institution or chaplain.

Corresponding with Inmates

KEY VERSE

These things I have written to you who believe in the name of the Son of God, that you may know that you have eternal life, and that you may continue to believe in the name of the Son of God.

1 John 5:13

INTRODUCTION

This chapter is for those who wish to be involved in a correspondence ministry with jail or prison inmates. It explains how to get started and presents guidelines for safe and effective correspondence.

HOW TO GET STARTED

First, contact the proper authorities at the institution. Some prisons provide programs that match inmates to "friends outside" for corresponding and/or visits. If the prison does not have such a program, contact the chaplain for names of those who need someone to write to them.

Second, obtain a list of the rules for corresponding with inmates at that specific prison. Most institutions have established written rules that govern correspondence. These differ from institution to institution. Some prisons permit you to send stamps and stationary through the mail, soft cover books, Gospel tracts, Bibles, and cassette tapes. Other institutions have specific procedures for sending such materials, i.e., the book must come directly from the publisher. Some institutions do not permit inmates to receive any of these items through the mail.

GUIDELINES FOR CORRESPONDING

Here are some guidelines to help you correspond effectively with inmates.

1. Keep in mind as you write to prisoners that many of them feel suspicious, resentful, and lonely.

- They are suspicious, because they have been abused or taken advantage of in past relationships. They may question your motive for writing: "What are you getting out of doing this?" Work at developing mutual trust, respect and understanding.
- Inmates are often resentful because they have been rejected by society, and after all, you too are a member of that society. Give inmates unconditional love and understanding.
- Inmates feel lonely because they are alienated from society, friends, and family. Many have been rejected by the latter. A week without a letter can seem like a year, so write often and respond promptly. One prisoner is reported to have called mail "paper sunshine."

2. Pray that God will help you to properly understand each letter and direct you with the proper response.

[1] My thanks to Dr. Patricia Hulsey for the majority of this section…used by permission.

3. If possible, it is best not to use your home address when answering letters. Use a post office box or your church or ministry address. This will avoid possible future problems, i.e., another inmate getting your home address, a parolee showing up unexpectedly on your door step, etc.

4. Make it clear from the beginning that you are not looking for romantic involvement. It is easy for prisoners to become

infatuated, even if they have never seen you, because of their loneliness. Kindness from you can be misinterpreted by them. If this happens, you should straighten it out in your very next letter or visit. Be courteous and tactful, but firm in this area. Some ministries restrict pen-pals to the same sex.

5. Do not share anything about yourself that can be used against you later, for any reason.
6. Do not send money unless you have really prayed about it and know God is directing you to do so. If you do send money, never loan it. Send it as an outright gift but make it clear not to expect future gifts. Be sure to clear the gift through proper channels at the institution.
7. Do not promise help with employment, housing, etc., after release from prison unless the ministry with which you are involved is adequately prepared to give it. Your purpose in writing is to be a source of encouragement in the Lord. Any request for social services should be channeled to proper post-prison release ministries.
8. Do not be too "preachy" in your letters. Establish relationship first, and then it is easy to share regarding spiritual matters. Share incidents from your everyday life that make the inmate feel part of your life and family.
9. Include in your letter anything you are permitted to send such as:
   - Photos, picture post cards.
   - Interesting news clippings.
   - Crossword or word search puzzles.
   - A gift of stamps or stationery, from time to time, if the institution permits.
   - Funny cartoons, paper book marks.
   - Bible studies or correspondence lessons.

VISITING INMATES

KEY VERSE

Remember the prisoners as if chained with them--those who are mistreated-- since you yourselves are in the body also.

Hebrews 13:3

INTRODUCTION

Many inmates in jails and prisons have no one to visit them:

1. Their family may live a great distance from where they are incarcerated or do not have the necessary transportation or finances to visit.
2. Their family may have rejected them, or they may have no family.
3. Former friends may have rejected them.

Personal visits with an inmate are one of the most rewarding areas of jail and prison ministry. This section explains its importance, details how to get involved, and offers guidelines for visiting individually with inmates.

THE IMPORTANCE OF PERSONAL VISITATION

Visiting an inmate on a one-on-one basis is an important ministry for the following reasons:

- Every soul is valuable to God: "The Lord is not willing that any should perish" (2 Peter 3:9). Jesus ministered to multitudes, but He always had time for the individual (for an example, see John 4).
- Many inmates will not attend religious services. Perhaps they have been "turned off" to the church by negative experiences. They may also be afraid that going to prison services will be interpreted as weakness by other inmates and make them vulnerable.

- Many inmates have never experienced true, Godly, unconditional friendship. They have only known abusive or impure relationships.
- As for most of us it is easier to open up in a personal rather than group setting. You can discuss many issues in a one-on-one visit that you cannot discuss in a group setting. The inmate can share personal needs with you, you can pray and study the Word together, and forge an intimate spiritual bond.
- You become a bridge back into society for the inmate. They will have a friend waiting when they are released from prison.
- One can't have too many friends. You will not only be a blessing, but you will be blessed by a true friendship with an inmate.

HOW TO GET INVOLVED

Here are some guidelines for how to get involved in one-on-one visitation with inmates.

- Inquire about the visitation program at the jail or prison where you want to volunteer. Many have an organized program for matching inmates with volunteers who want to visit one-on-one.
- If the institution does not have an organized program for matching inmates and visitors, ask the chaplain to match you with an inmate. If there is no chaplain, consult the administrator in charge of visitation and ask for a match.
- People who are ministering inside the prison on a group basis in religious programs are also a good source. They often know of inmates who have no one to visit them or who would benefit from personal attention.
- If possible, exchange a few letters with the inmate prior to your first visit. You will already feel like friends when you meet for the first time.

VISITATION GUIDELINES

Here are some visitation guidelines:

- Go through proper channels to be approved by the institution as a visitor. You may have to fill out certain forms, be pre-approved before your first visit, carry a specific type of identification, etc.
- Learn and abide by all rules for personal visitation in the institution where you are to visit. Rules may include issues like days and hours for visitation, appropriate dress, safety, and dress codes. They usually govern what can and cannot be taken into the institution with you. Many jails and prisons have their rules in writing. Ask for them.
- It is best to visit one-on-one with a person of your same sex. This avoids the pitfalls of improper romantic relationships.
- Normally, it is best not to give money to an inmate or their family. If you believe there is a legitimate need and you really believe God is directing you to do this, it is best to channel your help anonymously through the chaplain or another contact in the institution.
- If you forge a real friendship with an inmate, it will be easier to discuss spiritual matters and share the Gospel with them.
- Don't preach or lecture. Ask God to show you how to share His love and the Word of God in a way that will be accepted. After an inmate becomes a believer, continue to disciple him in the Word of God.
- If the institution permits, give a Bible and discipleship literature to your friend. Depending on institutional rules, you may be allowed to send these items through the mail, take them in yourself, or give materials to the chaplain to deliver.
- Unless you have had training, or you are gifted by God in the area of personal counseling, don't assume this role in the

relationship. You are there as a friend. Don't feel you must give an answer to every issue raised.
- As in any friendship, be a good confidant. Keep personal information shared by your special friend confidential.
- Prison is a very impersonal, dehumanizing place and an inmate doesn't have much opportunity to receive individual attention. Make your friend feel special. Make your visits a positive, uplifting, fun time.
- Always remember you are there as a representative of the Lord Jesus Christ—but don't spend all your time on spiritual matters. Foster a balanced relationship just as you do with your own personal friends. Discuss current events, laugh together, have fun with your friend!

CONDUCTING GROUP MEETINGS

Here are some general guidelines for conducting group services in a jail or prison.

TIMING

Correctional institutions are run on a strict schedule. All group meetings should begin and end on time.

MUSIC

Music for worship services in prison should be encouraging and uplifting. Songs that could be misunderstood by residents as condemning or as "put down" should not be used, e.g., "Rescue the Perishing." Neither should you use depressing music like "Nobody Knows The Trouble I've Seen." If you are using overhead transparencies, song books, or sound tracks, have these items ready. Always receive clearance from the chaplain before arranging musical activities which are different from that which your team normally does (special groups, cantatas, etc.).

PRAYER

Here are some suggestions for prayer time:

- Keep prayers short and to the point unless the Holy Spirit moves in a special way. A lengthy prayer could not only make the worship tedious but could be misunderstood by the prisoners.
- No particular position or posture is important, but when there is a large crowd (50 or more), it would be advisable to leave the congregation seated or standing while offering prayer rather than calling them forward to kneel. (This is for control purposes.)
- Spend most of the time praying for the physical, social, mental and spiritual welfare of inmates--their concerns and those relating to their families. Pray also for institutional staff.
- It is okay to keep your eyes open a bit (or have a member of your team designated to keep their eyes open) for control purposes.

SCRIPTURE READING

The person reading the Scripture, during a worship service, is "echoing" the voice of God and setting the tone for the sermon or lesson. Have the text read with expression, reverence and impressiveness (see Nehemiah 8:8). Announce clearly, before beginning to read, where the Scripture is located (book, chapter and verses). Allow time for those who have Bibles to find the passage. Project your voice to those in the back of the room. Stand erect and speak clearly. Read God's Word so impressively that the prisoners' emotions will be stirred, and their hearts turned heavenward.

TESTIMONIES

If you are asked to give a testimony, do not view this as your golden opportunity to preach. Do not use denominational jargon such as, "Since I came into the message" or "After I accepted the truth." It is better to use such phrases as "Since I became a Christian" or "After I accepted Jesus Christ as my personal Savior."

Keep your testimony Christ-centered and follow the ABC's of testifying:

A. Always tell what Christ has done for you and/or your family, telling things that are relevant to strengthening the faith of the prisoners. Don't glamorize sin by telling explicit details.
B. Be sure to keep it as short as possible, preferably 2-3 minutes. Don't try to tell it all. Remember that you are working in a scheduled time frame. The more you talk, the less time the speaker will have to deliver the Word.
C. Check your volume. Speak clearly and loudly, especially if no microphone is available, so you are heard and understood by all.

PREACHING OR TEACHING

Messages prepared for preaching or teaching in a prison should not exceed 30 minutes (unless, of course, the Holy Spirit is moving in some dramatic way). Many inmates have limited attention span. You also want to leave time enough at the end of your message so that you can conclude things properly and visit awhile with the residents (the fellowship is important to them).

Make your messages relevant to inmates. Adjust your presentation to what you know about your audience. Character building and encouragement messages are always good. When making a point about wrongdoing, always use "we" to include yourself.

The following things should never be done in a message:

- Never scold the residents. Enough of this has been received from relatives, lawyers, judges, etc.
- Never make statements that can be misinterpreted by prison staff as a breach of security.
- Never downgrade other religions.
- Never present a "holier than thou" attitude.
- Never ask antagonistic questions or assume the group disagrees with you.

- In small groups, wherever possible, use the circle seating arrangement.
- In small groups, encourage class participation. The question and answer method are effective.
- Don't let one person dominate the conversation.
- Make sure everyone has a Bible and encourage them to read along.
- If you must eject a disruptive student from a group, be tactful and courteous, but be firm. If necessary, get the cooperation of a correctional officer.

RESPONSE

If you ask for response from the group at the end of a message--to accept Christ as Savior or rededicate their lives--be very clear about exactly what you want them to do and why. If you have a large group, it is best to have them raise their hands rather than come forward (security precautions).

INMATE PARTICIPATION

Encourage inmates to be part of the service. For example, have an inmate sing a solo or share his testimony. Exercise caution about the content and length of inmate participation. Keep in mind that you are working within a set time frame and you can allow only a minimum amount of resident participation at each service. If necessary, have a "waiting list." Be sure to screen solos inmates want to sing, as some who are new believers may not pick appropriate music. Always maintain control. Do not let any inmate take control of the group meeting.

In small group meetings--especially Christian groups dealing with addictions--provide opportunity for all inmates to participate and share. You may be jarred by one inmate verbally attacking another in such sessions. Intervene by directing the group back to issues rather than dealing in personalities.

FOLLOW-UP

Inmates who indicate their acceptance of Jesus Christ as their personal Savior during an appeal at the close of a group meeting--or at any other time--should receive follow up care while still in the institution.

If possible, their names should be secured, and one copy given to the chaplain and another retained for you to follow up. Encourage them to attend Bible study sessions, Sunday services, and other opportunities offered in the institution.

If the institution provides a way for them to be baptized in water, they should receive instruction on this and opportunity to do so. (One prison has a horse watering trough which the chaplain fills with water for baptismal services.)

New converts will be like young children taking their first spiritual steps. Most of the time, their environment will be alien and opposed to their new beliefs. Constant support, encouragement and prayer are needed. They should:

- Be kept as spiritually active as possible by participating in worship services, Bible studies, and other Christian activities.
- Be given some responsibility in the ministry as soon as they are ready to accept it. Many are quite talented, and their appropriate talents should be utilized for God's service. A study of spiritual gifts will help them identify and begin to flow in the gifts God has given to them.
- Be encouraged to continue regular attendance at worship services and Bible study sessions.
- Be encouraged to develop friendships with other Christians within and without the institution. You may want to assign a "spiritual buddy" to each new convert. This person will visit and/or write the resident regularly, as well as keep in touch after his/her release from prison. If the prisoner with whom you are working is transferred to another institution, the

"spiritual buddy" can continue to write and provide encouragement and spiritual guidance. (Caution: Be sure the "spiritual buddy" is the same sex as the convert.)

ENTERING AND EXITING THE ROOM

It is important--especially in large groups--to have established procedures for entering and exiting the room to keep things orderly. Some institutions require inmates to sign in so there is a record of their participation. Assign some inmates to remain behind and put the room back in order: Erase boards, secure equipment, put up materials, pick up trash, and straighten chairs and tables.

MINISTERING TO INMATE'S FAMILIES

KEY VERSE

"And in you all the families of the earth shall be blessed."

Genesis 12:3

INTRODUCTION

Thousands of families are directly affected each year by having one of their loved ones incarcerated in a prison or jail. Most of these families are broken and filled with loneliness, anxiety, and feelings of rejection. Few of these families receive adequate attention from the church. God told Abraham that through him, "all the families of the earth shall be blessed." As spiritual heirs of Abraham, we too can bless families. This chapter explores ways you and/or your church can be involved in ministering to the families of inmates.

UNDERSTANDING THE CRISIS

When a family member is arrested, it usually creates anxiety, fear, and uncertainty for their mate, children, or parents. Imprisonment brings a double crisis to a family. The first crisis is that one of the family members has been arrested for breaking some law. The second crisis is that the family is split apart. Losing a family member to imprisonment is like the person dying. Children face shame and loss when a parent is in prison. They may be displaced, having to live with relatives, friends, foster homes, or in institutions. Many do not get to visit the incarcerated parent--perhaps because of court orders, distance from the prison, or the financial situation of those keeping them which prohibits visiting (costs for transportation, food, and housing).

HOW TO HELP INMATE'S FAMILIES

Here are some practical ways to minister to inmate's families:

Transportation and hospitality:

Provide transportation to and from the institution so the family can visit. If you live near a prison, provide a place for the family to stay overnight while visiting. Studies have shown that families that stay together and keep in touch with the member in prison have an important influence in helping that member readjust to society upon release.

Information

The family may not know how to get information--things like trial dates, when and how to visit, or how to obtain legal representation. You can be a help if you familiarize yourself with the system.

Social services

Share information on public and private agencies whose function is to provide employment, legal aid, housing, financial assistance, counseling, education, etc. The family may also need assistance in applying for these programs.

Employment

If the wage earner is incarcerated, the mate may need to find employment.

Housing, food, clothing, and finances

The family may need temporary or permanent housing, food, or finances to help get them on their feet. If you or your church provides financial help, checks should be used--if possible--and made out for the bills involved, directly to the landlord, utility companies, etc.

Counseling

The entire family or individual family members may need personal counseling in order to deal with the crisis.

Presents on special occasions: Christmas and birthdays are difficult for children and their incarcerated parent(s). One way you can help is to purchase gifts for Christmas and birthdays, wrap them, and present them to the child from the incarcerated parent. This cheers both inmate and child!

A church home

The most important thing you can do for an inmate's family is to provide a loving, supportive, accepting church home.

HOW TO CONTACT AN INMATE'S FAMILY

There are two important things you must do before contacting an inmate's family:

- Check with the chaplain or administration at the jail or prison where you are ministering. See if there are rules against this or an established procedure you should follow.
- Obtain written permission from the inmate so the family and institution know you have his/her approval. The request also clarifies the purpose for your contact.

A friendly telephone call or brief visit should initiate this ministry. At the culmination of the visit or call, offer a brief prayer. On the next visit, bring a copy of the same literature that the inmate is using for adult family members, so they can progress spiritually together. If they are not interested in the literature, then continue visiting on a strictly friendly and supportive basis. Always try to channel the conversation towards the present conditions of the home, family, employment, and plans for the future. Discourage attempts to dwell on negative aspects of the past. On subsequent visits, the family may share personal problems with you. If a basic need is obvious, tactfully inquire if you may be of assistance in filling it.

Note: Husband and wife teams are ideal visitors. Men should never visit an inmate's wife alone, nor should a woman visit an inmate's husband alone.

When you are working with an inmate's family, keep all personal matters confidential. Share only that which you have received specific permission from the incarcerated family member to reveal. Never get involved in legal matters or mention alleged problems between the prisoner and his/her family.

8

Post Prison Ministry

KEY VERSE

To open blind eyes, to bring out the prisoners from the prison, and them that sit in darkness out of the prison house.

Isaiah 42:7

INTRODUCTION

Some prisoners are released after serving their entire sentence as prescribed by law. In some legal jurisdictions, after completing part of their sentence, prisoners are eligible to go before a parole board. If granted parole before finishing their sentence, they are released with certain conditions, such as reporting regularly, not associating with ex-felons, and restrictions governing living and working arrangements. Conditions for release vary and are usually set by the court, a parole board, or a parole officer. Inmates being released from prison have many needs as they reenter society. This chapter will help you identify these needs, understand various types of post-prison ministries, and define your role in ministering to ex-offenders.

THE NEEDS OF THE EX-OFFENDER

Some inmates are blessed to be returning to supportive families or churches upon release from prison, but if they do not have such a support network then post-prison ministry is very important. Each person is different and has unique needs, but here are some common needs most ex-offenders share upon discharge from an institution.

- He/she needs to be accepted in a local church that is nurturing and supportive, so they can develop spiritually and

relationally. Invite him/her to go to church with you. Sit with them and invite them to have a meal or snack with you after service.
- He/she needs housing, food, and clothing. Inmates who have no "street clothes" sometimes need a "parole box", a box containing clothes, underwear, and shoes that he can wear when he leaves the institution grounds.
- She needs vocational training and/or a job. Where possible, helping the ex-offender to complete the Career Direct Profile can be a great blessing. For more information, see https://careerdirect-ge.org/my-business.
- He may need financial counseling # (basics of budgeting, maintaining personal finances, etc.) A special note: Don't give financial help personally to an ex-offender. It is better that financial assistance is channeled through your church or the administrators of a post-prison program.
- Family counseling is important if he is trying to reunite his family.
- He may need additional personal counseling for addictions like drugs and alcohol.
- Believers who have made a commitment to Christ may find addictive temptations one of their first spiritual battles on the outside.
- If he has been incarcerated for a long time, he may need assistance with even simple decisions because inmates have very limited options for making decisions in prison.
- He needs a strong support network of friends who will love and accept him, pray for and with him, and help him work through problems.

In addition, find out as much as possible about the inmate before release. This knowledge will assist in post-prison ministry. Determine his job skills and educational level. Find out where he is paroling to (sometimes it is required that an inmate go to a certain geographic location).

Discuss plans with the chaplain and the appropriate institution authorities before you speak to the inmate about it. Do not promise anything if you cannot follow through on it.

We highly recommend the book by DeKoven and Mills, Financial Integrity available from Vision Publishing.

POST-PRISON MINISTRIES

There are different types of post-prison ministries which you may want to start and/or to which an inmate can be referred:

- A Christian "half way house or Sober Living Program." This is a group home for ex-offenders and is called "half-way" because it is a transition between prison and getting back into normal society. This type of ministry usually provides housing, food, counseling, and job placement assistance to its residents. Participants may remain there for a set time dictated by authorities or until they find employment and housing. Some group homes have a discipleship program and participants are required to complete the program before moving out on their own. If you start a half-way house, it is important that you have strict rules concerning drugs, alcohol, curfews, and other general behavior standards.
- The local rescue mission: Some cities operate rescue missions that accept ex-offenders into their discipleship and vocational programs.
- Government or privately-operated programs: Some areas have government or privately-operated programs to help ex-offenders be integrated back into society. These may include group homes, vocational counseling, and other assistance.
- Church based programs: A local church may choose to start an ex-offenders group, offering assistance in housing, counseling, and job placement. Business owners in the church may be recruited to give an ex-felon a job. One church opened a fast-food restaurant that was run entirely by born-again ex-felons.

- Christian Colleges and Bible Schools: Some offer scholarships, room and board to promising ex-felons. If you are an administrator of a Christian college or Bible school, this would be a tremendous post-prison ministry to offer.

STARTING A POST PRISON MINISTRY

Here are five steps for starting a post-prison ministry:

STEP ONE: Pray

All things are fueled by prayer. Pray about what God would have you do in the area of post-prison ministries. Remember that this is not an easy area of ministry but can be abundantly fruitful for the Kingdom of God.

STEP TWO: Consult your spiritual leader

If you are a pastor, consult with your board. If you are a church member, talk with your pastor. This is important for several reasons:

1. It is common courtesy.
2. Spiritual leaders can guide and provide valuable input to you.
3. Your spiritual leader may already have plans underway for such a ministry. If so, be part of it, don't undermine it.
4. Do an analysis.

Here are some questions to answer in your analysis:

- Are there any local post-prison ministries? If so, what are they? (You may want to become part of a post-prison ministry already in existence.)
- What needs exist in your community regarding post-prison resources? This information is easy to come by, through reaching out to local law enforcement and also other ministries already serving in this area.

- What needs can you and/or your church fill? (Try not to duplicate efforts of other Christian organizations. We should complement, not compete with one another.)

STEP FOUR: Visit a similar ministry

If you decide to start a post-prison ministry, visit a similar ministry that exists elsewhere. Learn from their successes and failures.

STEP FIVE: Determine organizational issues

Here are some organizational issues to determine:

- Funding
  - Post-prison ministries need financial resources. Determine how funds will be secured and develop an operating budget. Your church may be in a position to help, but generally not, as they are looking for funds as well.
- Facilities
  - What type of facility is needed? Where will it be located? Can you get required approvals by the local government to locate the facility in the area you are considering?
- Staffing
  - Who will run the post-prison ministry? What are the necessary qualifications? Will the positions be paid or volunteer?

DETERMINING YOUR ROLE

What will your role be in post-prison ministry? It depends on the answer to the following questions:

- What is permitted by the institution in which you minister? Some institutions prohibit volunteers who minister inside the prison from working with inmates after their release. They reason that should the inmate return to prison, they might be

too familiar with the volunteer or be shown special favors because of their relationship outside the institution.
- Where are you most effective? Are you more effective ministering to inmates inside or upon release from prison? Where does your interest and vision lie? Which gives you the greatest joy and the greatest spiritual results?
- What are your time and energy limitations? You can't be everything to everyone. Due to personal time and energy restraints, you may need to confine yourself to ministering to inmates either inside or upon release, but not both.

If your institution does not permit your involvement with inmates upon release or you do not have the time or burden for post-prison ministries, then you will want to serve only as a referral agent.

Make a list of churches, individuals, or Para-church organizations involved in post-prison ministries and refer inmates to them.

Whatever your involvement, your role should be that of a friend and facilitator. Don't become a crutch for the inmate. Be available, but don't smother him/her. Encourage self-reliance.

Institutional and Inmate Typology

KEY VERSE

The spirit of the Lord God is upon me; because the Lord hath anointed me to preach good tidings unto the meek; he hath sent me to bind up the brokenhearted, to proclaim liberty to the captives, and the opening of the prison to them that are bound.

Isaiah 61:1

INTRODUCTION

Are some inmates considered more dangerous than others? Are there any differences between a jail and a prison? Do inmates share any common characteristics? How do you respond to someone who maintains their innocence? These are key issues that are addressed in this section.

INSTITUTIONAL TYPOLOGY

Each jail and prison is unique, but most institutions are classified by the type of inmates they house.

- Maximum security institutions
  - These house inmates that are the greatest risk, perhaps due to the nature of their crime or their behavior in prison. Death rows are usually located in maximum security institutions. These inmates have very close supervision and their participation in institutional programs run by volunteers is sometimes restricted.
- Medium security institutions
  - These house less violent inmates who do not pose a great security or escape risk. They do not require as much supervision and may be allowed to freely participate in religious programs.
- Minimum security institutions
  - These are composed of inmates who are close to their release date, incarcerated for non-violent crimes, or those who have proven themselves to be extremely reliable and trustworthy. They may even work outside the prison on occasion and usually have freedom to participate in religious programs.

Some institutions house all three security levels in various areas of the same facility. Each of these levels are often found in jails as well. Institutions sometimes clothe the inmates in uniforms of differing colors to identify the various security levels.

DIFFERENCES BETWEEN JAILS AND PRISONS

Although jails and prisons both house offenders, there are differences between the two. Prison inmates have been tried and convicted. Jail is usually the entry point for all prisoners. Many jail inmates haven't been convicted of anything yet. Most are being held pending trial. Some are being held pending sentencing. Some may be serving sentences so brief that it doesn't warrant sending them to a prison.

Prison population is relatively stable. People serve longer terms, so you have more time to work with them. Jail population is very transient. People are held in jails only while awaiting trial, sentencing, or serving brief sentences. Your time with them is limited.

Some prisons have at least a minimum of facilities and programs for counseling and rehabilitation, but most jails have few or none. Prisons usually have better facilities for group meetings such as church services and group Bible studies.

The physical, emotional, and psychological conditions of jail inmates are different from and less favorable than those in prisons. There is usually no privacy in which to talk with individual inmates in jails. The prisoners in jails are often bored, restless, and fearful. Most of all, uncertainty rules their lives.

OTHER TYPES OF FACILITIES

Other types of programs of confinement include:
- Work release centers
  - Allow an inmate to hold a job in the community during the day and return to the center for confinement at night.
- Halfway house
  - For persons on parole. They are required to stay at the house while seeking employment and a permanent place to live. They may be required to complete certain counseling or training programs offered at the halfway house.
- Road camp, fire camp, forestry camp, or work farm
  - Inmates work on roads, fight fires, or work on public forests or a farm.

- Detention, juvenile hall, or reformatory
  - Typically for young offenders to be kept separate from older prisoners.

Despite the distracting environment, jails, prisons, and other penal programs are some of the greatest spiritual harvest fields in the world. Jesus only had a few minutes with the dying thief on the cross, but his entire destiny was changed for all eternity.

INMATE TYPOLOGY

Each inmate is unique. God loves each one and is not willing that any should perish. There is no "typical" inmate in God's sight, but there are some common characteristics that will help you understand the majority.

Education

Often, the educational level of inmates is low.

Home environment

Inmates often come from homes where there was abuse, divorce, little supervision, and no discipline.

Vocational training

Many inmates have little or no vocational training. They may have been unsuccessful at obtaining or maintaining employment or labored at low paying jobs.

Self-image

Inmates often have low self-image because they have been rejected by society, friends, or family.

Emotional profile

Many inmates suffer from guilt over what they have done or put their families through. Depression, hopelessness, and hostility are common, which are often precursors to drug and alcohol abuse.

Social responsibility: Inmates sometimes have a limited sense of social responsibility. They may feel no remorse for their crime or that they got a "bad break" from the system by coming to prison.

Common Offenses

Four crimes account for the majority of prison inmates in most countries: Robbery, burglary, murder, and narcotics violations. Other common reasons for incarceration are sexual offenses, kidnaping, assault, embezzlement, forgery, and fraud.

Inmates also assume various roles in prison that you should be aware of in ministry:

- "Hecklers" may come to a Bible class as earnest students and then disrupt by asking unanswerable questions. They may try to pour out scandalous stories about the church and ministers or turn testimony time into a gripe session. Maintain control of group sessions by continually bringing the group back to the subject at hand.
- Perennial seekers respond to every altar call due to a lack of understanding of what conversion is all about, a desire to please you, or because they have lived like a sinner since they last responded. Continue to receive them warmly when they respond and pray with them. When they are secure in their relationship with God and really understand conversion, they will change.
- Manipulators are those who may be charming and agreeable but try to use you to accomplish their own purposes.
- Institutionalized inmates are those who have been confined for a lengthy period of time and have difficulty functioning apart from an institutional setting. If they return to prison after paroling, don't be discouraged. They may be sincere in their confession of the Lord but just need more skills for adjusting to life outside.

Remember, these characteristics are not true of all inmates. Some are very educated and held high paying jobs. Some came from good homes and supportive families. Some are sincere seekers, desiring to learn about God. These general characteristics are based on numerous studies of the majority of prison inmates.

Most important, remember to view each inmate not as they were, or even as they are. View them as the valiant men and women of God that they will become when the Gospel has supernaturally impacted their lives!

ARE SOME REALLY INNOCENT?

Many inmates maintain their innocence. For some who are actually guilty, this can be an escape mechanism. They cannot face what they did, so they rationalize or blame others. But please—be aware--some inmates who maintain their innocence actually are innocent! There have been many cases where inmates were released from prison after it was proven--beyond a doubt—that they were wrongly convicted. (This applies to former death row inmates also!)

You are not there to judge the guilt or innocence of an inmate. You are there to be a friend and minister God's love to them. Be supportive. Tell them you will pray for God to undertake in their case and for justice to be done.

Remember that—for various reasons—many heroes of the faith ended up with prison records.

Joseph spent at least two years in prison after he was falsely accused of attempted rape (Genesis 39). Samson was imprisoned by the Philistines (Judges 16). Jeremiah was put into King Zedekiah's dungeon twice, once for unpopular preaching and once when falsely accused of treason (Jeremiah 32, 37).

Many of the apostles were thrown into prison by the Sadducees (Acts 5). Herod imprisoned John the Baptist (Matthew 4) and Peter (Acts 12), as well as Paul. The apostle Paul had a lengthy prison record. He served sentences in Jerusalem (Acts 23), in Caesarea (Acts 23), a local jail in Philippi (Acts 16), and probably two different times in a prison in Rome.

Christians have been imprisoned throughout church history--John Bunyan and Dietrich Bonhoeffer are two most notable believers who were incarcerated. Modern China, Russia, and Uganda have seen thousands of believers imprisoned and martyred.

Jesus said that being a faithful Christian may lead to prison (Matthew 10 and 24). Conversely, being a prisoner may also lead to faith--as one death row inmate discovered on Calvary.

Always remember there are great men and women of faith on both sides of the prison wall.

CONCLUSION

But the Word of God is not bound.

2 Timothy 2:9

Jesus is in your local jail. He is doing time in prison.

"Then the righteous will answer Him, saying, `Lord, when did we see You in prison, and come to You?' And the King will answer and say to them, `Assuredly, I say to you, inasmuch as you did it to one of the least of these My brethren, you did it to Me.'"

Matthew 25:37-40

From a spiritual standpoint, there is no value that can be placed on the soul of a man, woman, or young person.

"For what profit is it to a man if he gains the whole world, and loses his own soul? Or what will a man give in exchange for his soul?"

Matthew 16:26

From a purely financial standpoint, every person kept out of prison saves thousands of dollars a year in direct costs for incarceration. This doesn't include the social service expenses for their families provided by some governments, nor does it calculate the tremendous human costs to the family or economic contributions the prisoner would make if gainfully employed.

By accepting the mandate for jail and prison ministries--by marching fearlessly past the rows of razor wire and armed guard posts--you are going into the very depths of hell to mine precious gems for the Lord.

Oh yes, there will be some who do not receive your message. There will be others who will profess, but not really possess. There will be some who return to their old ways. But remember:

- God started with a man and woman with a perfect heritage who lived in a perfect environment, and both of them failed.
- When Jesus revealed that He must suffer, many disciples ceased to follow Him--they were not willing to pay the cost.
- In His final hours, His remaining disciples fled, one denied Him, and one betrayed Him--yet several of these men fulfilled the great challenge of taking the Gospel to the nations of the world.

Do not measure the worth of jail and prison ministries by your failures. Measure its worth by your successes. You are part of a world-wide network that is changing the world--One jail and prison at a time, one person at a time.

There are many challenges to jail and prison ministry, but there are also tremendous rewards. Volunteers often start working with inmates and ex-offenders thinking, "I'll go into this dark place and take the love of God." Very often, they come out testifying, "I got more than I gave."

By accepting the mandate of jail and prison ministry you become part of an exciting team—a world-wide network of volunteers who are gathering up jewels for the Master.

> "They shall be Mine," says the LORD of hosts, "On the day that I make them My jewels. And I will spare them as a man spares his own son who serves him."
>
> Malachi 3:17

Continue to raise up spiritual sons and daughters until the Master returns.

- Don't ever be discouraged.
- Don't ever lose the vision.
- Don't ever give up on an inmate.
- Don't ever quit.

> *"Lift up your eyes all around, and see: they all gather together, they come to you; your sons shall come from afar, and your daughters shall be nursed at your side."*
>
> Isaiah 60:4

Other Chaplaincy Services

The Funeral Service

Introduction

I (Dr. Stan) have often said I prefer funerals to weddings, for with a funeral you know the outcome, but with a wedding only the Lord knows.

In conducting a funeral as a chaplain, you may or may not have much knowledge of the family or even the person who is now dead. As in all areas of ministry, sensitivity is needed and planning is helpful. You really never know what you will be facing, so we have presented here some guidelines we hope will help.

The Funeral or Memorial Service

As with all areas of ministry, it begins with proper preparation; spiritual and natural. From a natural view point, you will want to make sure you have a well-planned service to meet the needs of the family. Spiritually, recognize your role; you are a spiritual advisor, and this is a spiritual moment for the family, so be prepared to pray, to give brief counsel, care and comfort as a part of your duties in directing the funeral. Thus, you will want to consult with the family, and respond to their specific requests to the best of your ability.

Service outline

(see sample services in the appendix section).

1. Start with Scripture
2. A singer can bring a song or a hymn
3. Obituary
4. Prayer
5. One more song or hymn
6. Message
7. Benediction
- As you close the service approach the coffin and wait for the family.

The Burial

If you are called upon to officiate the actual burial of a loved one, you will want to keep some things in mind as you spend time with family and friends after the service. You will want this portion of the process of letting go of the loved one to be brief, but also meaningful. Remember, the family is still be grieving, and the burial is the final reminder of the permanence of their loss. Thus, after the burial, you should make it a point if possible, to call or visit them after the funeral service. Finally, don't preach to them; instead give them words of consolation.

The Grief Experience

Chaplains often serve best in the middle of the grieving process for family and friends. To follow are the stages of grief that are commonly referred to in professional circles. However, remember that no two people grieve exactly the same. For an extensive study on grief and loss, and the process of recovery, see Dr. Stan DeKoven's Grief Relief, available through Vision Publishing (www.booksbyvision.org).

Stages of Grief
(modified from Kubler-Ross)

- Shock - a sense of suspended believe that the loss has actually happened.
- Denial - similar to shock but longer lasting, where the person suspends the true knowledge of loss due to the pain experienced.
- Fantasy vs. Reality - some call this bargaining, but really, it is an attempt to cope with the loss and is often filled with flash backs to previous conversations, dreams that seem so real that the person is still alive, etc.
- Release - expression of repressed emotions connected to thoughts. This begins the process of recovery.
- Living with memories - the good, bad and ugly, and putting them in their proper place.
- Acceptance and affirmation - that life is still worth living, and God is indeed good.

General Process of Grief Relief

In my 40 plus years of counseling, I have used this simple three-word outline to help people and counselors (including many Chaplains) to focus their ministry for those suffering loss. They are:

- Admit - One's life has changed permanently due to their loss, and that they can and will make it through by God's grace. Proverbs 28:13, Psalm 19:12, Psalm 90:8
- Submit - to the often painful process of change, which is inevitable, and has truly manifested in times of loss. Joel 2:12, Hebrews 12:5, 1 John 1:9, Matthew 18:1-6
- Commit - to making small, incremental changes over time, under the guidance of the chaplain, counselor or pastor. Ezekiel 18:31, Psalm 37:5

Principles for Overcoming Loss

Grief is the natural healing process that occurs after a significant loss. It is experienced uniquely by each of us, often in waves, with emotional, cognitive, physical and social responses varying in terms of the intensity.

Emotional components of loss can include:

- Shock, numbness, feeling of unreality
- Helplessness
- Vulnerability
- Fearfulness
- Sadness
- Anger, irritability
- Guilt
- Carelessness, harming oneself or others
- Outbursts, euphoria
- Cognitive components of loss can include:
- Slowed and/or disorganized thinking
- Confusion, aimlessness, difficulty concentrating
- Preoccupation, rumination
- Unaffected, no thoughts at all about the person or the circumstances
- Dreams
- Decreased self-esteem
- Altered perceptions, sensing the presence of the deceased person
- Physical components of loss can include:
- Fatigue, sleep disturbance
- Decreased or increased appetite
- Physical distress, nausea
- Anxiety, hypo- or hyperactivity
- Greater susceptibility to illness
- Social components of loss include:
- Being unaware of others' needs
- Passivity
- Withdrawing from or avoiding others
- Decreased work productivity

- Loss of interest in usual pleasures, including hobbies and/or relationships
- Strained relationships, difference in grieving needs between self and others.
- Variables that can affect a grief reaction:
- Your own history of past losses, through deaths, divorce, relocation, lost dreams, phase of life changes
- Violations of one's safety (accidents, fire, personal trauma, world crises), or health changes
- Your current personal and situational stressors
- Your personal beliefs in a faith tradition or spiritual practice
- Your cultural and family expectations about loss
- If the loss is anticipated or unanticipated
- If the loss is marked by traumatic events
- The degree to which closure with the person was possible
- A "loss out of season," for the person who has died or for you
- Your ability to share the loss with others
- Your coping style and use of stress management resources
- Working through past hurts and forgiveness issues
- Finding a way to make meaning of the loss

The Purpose of Grief and Mourning

Yes, it does have a purpose, and it is going somewhere. Grief responses are natural reactions.

- Your feelings about the loss
- Your protest at the loss and your wish to undo it and have it not be true.
- The affects you experience from the assault which is caused by the loss

The ultimate goal of grief is to take you beyond these reactions to the loss.

Working Actively On Adapting To It

The therapeutic purpose of grief and mourning is to get you to the point where you can live with the loss healthily, after having made the necessary changes to do so.

What must you do to get to this point? You must:

- Change your relationship with your loved one.
- Develop a new sense of yourself to reflect the changes
- Take on healthy new ways of being in the world without your loved one.
- Find new people, objects or pursuits, emotional investment. This will help you recognize that your loved one is gone and then to make the necessary internal (psychological) & external (social) changes to accommodate this reality.

Learning to Live Healthily with Your Loss

Rate yourself on each one as to whether or not "I am here now," "I am having a little difficulty with this," or "I can't do this yet."

- You have returned to your normal levels of psychological, social and physical functioning in all realms of your life.
- There is a general decline in all your symptoms of grief.
- You are not overwhelmed by emotions in general or whenever the loss is mentioned.
- You are back to your normal level of self-esteem.
- You can enjoy yourself without feeling guilty, and you don't feel guilty for living.
- Your hatred and anger, if any, doesn't consume you and is not directed inappropriately at others.
- You do not have to restrict your emotions and thoughts to avoid confronting something painful.
- It is not that you don't hurt, but the hurt now is limited, manageable, and understood.
- You appreciate how you are similar to and different from other bereaved persons.

- You do not have to obsess about nor think solely of the deceased and the death.
- You feel that you have done what you needed to do, either to atone for your guilt or to learn to live with it.
- You lead the pain, it doesn't lead you.
- You can appreciate the bittersweet quality of certain experiences, such as holidays and special events in which you feel the sweetness of those who are around you as well as the sadness of not being with your deceased loved one.
- You are able to meet and cope with secondary losses in a healthy fashion.
- You don't become anxious when you have nothing to do. You don't have to be occupied all the time to be without tension.
- You can remember pain, and you can talk about the deceased and the death without crying.
- You no longer feel exhausted, burdened, or wound up all the time.
- You can find some meaning in life.
- You do not have to hold time, or yourself, back.
- You have "accepted" the loss in the sense of not fighting the fact that it happened.
- You are comfortable with your new identity and the new adjustments you have made to accommodate being without your loved one in the world. Though you wouldn't have chosen to have to change, you are not fighting it now.
- You are comfortable with the emotions that temporarily are aroused when you occasionally bump the scar from your losses (for example, at anniversaries or special events). You know how to deal with the grief and you understand that it is normal.
- You know how and when to take time to mourn.
- You can look forward to and make plans for the future.

- You have a healthy perspective on what your grief resolution will and will not mean for you.
- You are not inappropriately closed down in your feelings, relationships, or approaches to life. For example, you do not overprotect yourself or fail to take any risks.
- You can let the world go on now without feeling it has to stop because your loved one has died.
- You can deal with others' insensitivity to your loss without becoming unduly distressed or overemotional.
- You are regaining interest in people and things outside of yourself or which don't pertain to your lost loved one.
- You can put the death in some perspective.

There may be other signs that would indicate to you that you now are learning to live with your loss in as healthy a fashion as possible. The ones listed here will give you some examples of the ways in which resolution and recovery can be shown. You will note that none of them suggest that you not have some connection with your deceased loved one, or that you forget that person. They all center on learning to live with the fact of your loved one's absence, moving forward in the world despite the fact that the scar will remain and, on occasion, bring pain.

In the end, this moving forward with the scar is the very best that we could hope for. You would not want to forget your loved one, as if she has never existed or not been an important part of your life.

Learning to Live with the Loss in Terms of Your Relationship with the Deceased

- You can realistically remember the good and the bad, the happy and the sad of both the deceased and your relationship.
- Any identification you have with the deceased is healthy and appropriate.

- You can forget the loss for a while without feeling like you are betraying your loved one.
- You have a comfortable and healthy new relationship with the deceased, with appropriate withdrawal of emotional energy but also appropriate ways to keep that person "alive."
- You are able to stop "searching" for your lost loved one.
- You do not have to hold on to the pain to have a connection with your deceased loved one.
- The rituals that keep you connected to your loved one are acceptable to you and healthy.
- You can concentrate on something besides your deceased loved one.
- In your relationship with your deceased loved one, you have achieved healthy amounts of holding on and letting go.

Learning to Live with the Loss in Terms of Adjusting to the New World

- You have integrated the loss into your ongoing life. You are able to relate to others in a healthy fashion and to work and function at the same level as before.
- You can accept the help, support, and condolences of others.

"To name a thing is to tame it."

On a daily basis we can do things like this:

- Taking sufficient time off from work
- Eating as well as you can
- Drinking water
- Loafing and resting
- Moving our bodies- a walk, bike ride, swimming
- Getting massages
- Listening to music
- Simplifying our schedules
- Cutting out activities that take up time and energy we don't now have
- Praying and meditating

- Talking to a professional

Comfort Quickies: Self Care While Grieving

It is common to need breaks from our emotions. These ideas may give you some additional nourishment to respond to the stress that comes with grieving.

- Lie in the sun streaming in through your windows. Bathe, breathe in the sun.
- Designate an afternoon or evening and take the phone off the hook.
- When you are worried or obsessing, set up a specific time of the day to "worry" for 20 minutes. Set a timer. When the time is up, do something rewarding for yourself.
- Do something you're good at. It is important to ground yourself in your skills and abilities; even if the outcome isn't up to par (trouble concentrating, and decreased zest are common in grief).
- Comfort yourself by taking a warm bath using your favorite scents and burn aromatherapy candles. It's invigorating and relaxing at the same time.
- Buy yourself or your loved one a gift—and have the clerk gift wrap it. Choose the prettiest paper and bow. Celebrate fond memories.
- Wrap up in a warm blanket. Put on relaxation tapes and sip your favorite tea or hot chocolate.
- Dressed in comfortable clothing, find a rocking chair and rock your troubles away.
- Play music that matches your mood. Feel understood by the songs and singers that share your experiences.
- Especially when you are feeling stressed and overwhelmed, forget about making to-do lists. Instead, at the close of each day, make a list of what's been done.
- Find something alive to care for, such as a plant or a pet.

- Eat at least one nourishing meal each day, even if the food doesn't hit your taste buds like you're used to.
- Say "No" to something… and "Yes" to yourself.
- Make a fire in the fireplace and do some stretching and focus on yourself. You can add your favorite soft music to this, if you wish.
- Breathe—really breathe! Take deep breaths in through the nose and slowly out through the mouth.
- Spend some time in nature.
- Make a memory box, collage, or journal to store your thoughts and memories.

Creatively Coping with Grief

It really is a process. Some things that might help:

- Music
- Writing
- Plays and Video
- Watch a movie
- Buy a tree or plant, then create a ceremony to plant it
- Look for activities at your local recreation department or community college
- Join a health club, YMCA or local park and recreation department for exercise classes
- See a play or a concert at a high school or college. Check your local paper for listings and ideas
- Attend a church service
- Attend a poetry reading
- Start a journal to record your thoughts, feelings and writings—to share or just to get out of your system.
- Try to keep a cheerful disposition with sales clerks, people waiting in lines, people in the produce section of the grocery store, etc.
- Simple, genuine statements can often lead to conversations. For example, "I need to pick a present for my [fill in the

blank]. What do you think of this?" or "What a handsome dog!"
- Keep trying. You may find someone else who is experiencing the blues and would welcome the chance to talk with a pleasant stranger and may become a new friend.

9

The Chaplain's Role in Situations of Abuse

Key Verse

But as for me, I trust in You, O LORD, I say, "You are my God." My times are in Your hand; Deliver me from the hand of my enemies and from those who persecute me. Make Your face to shine upon Your servant; Save me in Your loving kindness.

Psalms 31:14-16

The Spirit of the Lord GOD is upon me, Because the LORD has anointed me To bring good news to the afflicted; He has sent me to bind up the brokenhearted To proclaim liberty to captives and freedom to prisoners. To proclaim the favorable year of the LORD And the day of vengeance of our God; To comfort all who mourn. To grant those who mourn in Zion, Giving them a garland instead of ashes, the oil of gladness instead of mourning, The mantle of praise instead of a spirit of fainting. So they will be called oaks of righteousness, The planting of the LORD, that He may be glorified.

Isaiah 61:1-3

WHAT IS ABUSE?

Abuse can be: Physical, Emotional, Psychological, Verbal, Financial, or Spiritual

Domestic violence is about power and control!

Whoever has the power abuses the person who has no power!

Who are the victims? Some statistics:

- 91-95% of all documented cases of domestic violence are against women.
- Domestic violence occurs in all classes and groups: Financial, educational, employment, physical ability, married, single, races, ethnicities.

Abuse is something you learn!

There is no excuse:

- No Alcohol - No Anger
- No Mental Illness - No Problems

Abusers plan their abuse!

Who is the abuser? Characteristics of abusers:

- 75% of abusers were abused
- Or witnessed abuse in their homes
- Do not trust others
- They are very jealous
- They isolate their spouses from their family and friends
- Abuse drugs or alcohol
- They are very dominant
- They are violent inside and outside the home

They are:

- Doctors
- Lawyers
- Police/Correction Officers
- Workers
- Pastors
- Lay ministers
- Rich
- Poor

How to identity abusive personalities:
- Jealousy
- Controlling of others
- Gets involved in relationships or marries quickly
- Unrealistic expectations
- Solitary
- Blame others for their problems
- They are very sensitive
- Abuse animals or children
- They have abused someone in the past
- Threaten
- Break things
- Forceful when arguing
- Super religious

What do victims feel?
- Fear
- Loneliness
- Hopelessness
- Powerlessness
- Anger

How Should A Christian Behave?

In Genesis we read that "God" created man and separated the male from the female. And He gave them both the Garden of Eden. When man sinned, he brought the punishment that included a curse to Eve that her desire would be for her husband. When Christ came, He restored the relationship between husband and wife. To God we are all His children. There is neither male nor female. The difference is something carnal. We must show mutual respect.

Husbands love your wives.

Ephesians 5:25-31, 33

How Can We Help?

Planning For Your Safety

A chaplain can help by:

- Breaking the silence and allowing the victim to talk.
- Recommending they seek a support group.
- Not forcing, disputing, accusing, or blaming the victim.
- Not telling the person that he/she should leave; allow the person to make that decision.
- Asking if he/she has a plan. (Simple Plan).
- Giving comfort and praying for the victim. Preparing scriptures to share and by listening.
- Providing literature that can comfort the victim—biblical literature, DVD material, and so on.

Comfort for Victims

> *But I trusted in thee, O LORD: I said, "Thou art my God. My times are in thy hand: deliver me from the hand of mine enemies, and from them that persecute me. Make thy face to shine upon thy servant: save me for thy mercies' sake."*
>
> Psalm 31:14-16

How Can We Help?

- Comforting
- Praying for her and her family
- Praying with her and other sisters
- Taking the hand of this sister
- Allowing her to cry and to vent

The Offender Is Responsible

Abuse is a crime; a crime against the innocent, those who are weak. We should not blame, but we must lead the sinner to repent and change his life. Do not fall into the traps of the sinners who seek to justify his actions. He has to accept that he is guilty and assume responsibility for the situation he created. He can only change when he confesses his sin and allows the Spirit of God to work in him. Sometimes, even though God forgives them, they do not want to change, and many abusers continue abusing. That's why we have a legal system that was established to bring the justice of man and God, to those who break the law.

God Is Opposed To Those Who Abuse People

> *O LORD my God, in thee do I put my trust: save me from all them that persecute me, and deliver me: Lest he tear my soul like a lion, rending it in pieces, while there is none to deliver. O LORD my God, if I have done this; if there be iniquity in my hands;*
>
> *If I have rewarded evil unto him that was at peace with me; (yea, I have delivered him that without cause is mine enemy:) Arise, O LORD, in thine anger, lift up thyself because of the rage of mine enemies: and awake for me to the judgment that thou hast commanded.*
>
> *The LORD shall judge the people: judge me, O LORD, according to my righteousness, and according to mine integrity that is in me. Oh let the wickedness of the wicked come to an end; but establish the just: for the righteous God trieth the hearts and reins. My defense is of God, which saveth the upright in heart. God judgeth the righteous, and God is angry with the wicked every day.*
>
> Psalm 7:1-4, 6, 8-11 KJV

Police, Courts and Protective Orders

What is a Protective Order?

A protective order is a court order. It may be a limited or full order—the abuser cannot come near the victim's home or employment.

Police have an arrest warrant when a protective order is in place. Where Can You Get A Protection Order?

- Family Court - Settlement
- The Criminal Court - Criminal

There is hope for the victims and forgiveness for the sinner. There are programs for the abuser and the victim; both can get help.

The responsibility of a minister or any believer is to help people find God or restore the relationship with God if they have strayed. The abuser may be led through a process of confession and repentance, but do not think this will be the end. Abuse is a situation that requires much prayer and both people involved need help, so they can continue with their lives. Healing takes time and effort. Some marriages or other relationships cannot be restored, especially if either one does not want to continue. If necessary, seek professional help.

A Prayer - Asking for Help

Give ear to my prayer, O God; and hide not thyself from my supplication.

Attend unto me, and hear me: I mourn in my complaint, and make a noise;

Because of the voice of the enemy, because of the oppression of the wicked:

for they cast iniquity upon me, and in wrath they hate me.

My heart is sore pained within me: and the terrors of death are fallen upon me.

Fearfulness and trembling are come upon me, and horror hath overwhelmed me.

And I said, Oh that I had wings like a dove! for then would I fly away, and be at rest.

Lo, then would I wander far off, and remain in the wilderness. Selah.

I would hasten my escape from the windy storm and tempest

For it was not an enemy that reproached me; then I could have borne it

neither was it he that hated me that did magnify himself against me; then

I would have hid myself from him:

But it was thou, a man mine equal, my guide, and mine acquaintance.

He hath put forth his hands against such as be at peace with him:

he hath broken his covenant.

The words of his mouth were smoother than butter, but war was in his heart:

his words were softer than oil, yet were they drawn swords.

Psalms 55:1-8, 12-13, 20-21 KJV

Why Did God Allow This To Happen?

Some ask: Why did this happen? Why was I abused? Why did God let this happen to me?

Like Job we cry in anguish. But shout in victory:

"Though he slay me, yet will I trust in him."

Job 13:15

The enemy brought the suffering in the life of Job. But God allows all these things to work for good. Like Job, we can grow as believers to help others who suffer so that God will be glorified. As followers of Jesus we carry our cross and we know that our reward will be more glorious than our suffering.

Why has God allowed this? The world is in crisis and requires women of courage, women who do not fear what the world or the devil brings their way. We have to rescue souls from the devil's hands and we cannot be cowards. He, who has received many beatings from life, can resist even more. Glory to God!

SEEKING HEALING AND DELIVERANCE

How can we receive our healing? Brethren, if you want your healing you must pursue it like the woman with the issue of blood. She had spent all her money, perhaps had visited the best doctors, and she still ended with her issue unresolved. In all the world, she couldn't find anyone who could help her. But when she heard of Jesus, she overcame her sense of shame and risked everything for her healing.

Seeking deliverance. We also need to be freed from the demons that plague us. We need to be delivered from wounded emotions, personal hang ups, bad attitudes, anger, and so on.

We must forgive our abusers. Without forgiveness we cannot receive our complete healing.

Prayer for Wounded Emotions

Father, in Jesus' name I come to you, feeling shame and my emotions wounded. I confess my transgressions (confess all past transgressions and those that the Holy Spirit reveals to you). You are faithful to forgive me and cleanse me from all unrighteousness. You are my refuge, O Lord, preserve me from trouble. You surround me with songs and shouts of deliverance. I have chosen life and according to Your word you saw me as I was being formed in my mother's womb. On the authority of Your Word that says that I was beautifully and wonderfully made, I now give myself to you to do your work in me in Christ Jesus.

Father, you have not given me the spirit of fear and I'm not ashamed. You gave me beauty for ashes, the oil of gladness instead of mourning and beautiful garments for the spirit of heaviness; that I might be a tree of righteousness, the planting of the Lord, that Christ is glorified.

I chose to forgive all who have hurt me in any way. YOU do not forsake me while I complete the process of forgiveness. I take comfort, I am encouraged and I say, "Surely, the Lord is my refuge, I will not be taken by surprise. What can man do to me?" This hope will never disappoint me, it's not deceiving, and it won't put me to shame because the love of God has been poured into my heart by the Holy Spirit.

I acknowledged my sin unto thee, and mine iniquity have I not hid. I said, I will confess my transgressions unto the LORD; and thou forgavest the iniquity of my sin. Selah.

For this shall every one that is godly pray unto thee in a time when thou mayest be found: surely in the floods of great waters they shall not come nigh unto him.

Thou art my hiding place; thou shalt preserve me from trouble; thou shalt compass me about with songs of deliverance. Selah.

Psalms 32:5-7 RV95

10

The Chaplain as Counselor

A Holy Calling

What is our purpose for all of us who exercise one or various ministries?

The Christian Ministry Vocation

This must be considered separately. One must understand that being a chaplain is as much a calling as it is a profession. The chaplaincy involves a few phases of work. As a servant of God, the chaplain is also:

- Counselor
- Preacher

How?

- He shares the message
- His personal testimony
- Promotes and encourages
- Tries to resolve difficult situations and spiritual needs

How do we know that we are called?

To do a good work as chaplains we must be sure that we were chosen by God.

In John 15:16 the Lord said, "You did not choose Me but I chose you, and appointed you that you would go and bear fruit, and that your fruit would remain, so that whatever you ask of the Father in My name He may give to you."

In Acts 26:16, the Lord spoke to Saul of Tarsus, who was on his way to Damascus: "But get up and stand on your feet; for this purpose I have appeared to you, to appoint you a minister and a witness not only to the things which you have seen, but also to the things in which I will appear to you;"

Five Historical Functions of Pastoral Ministry

1. Healing: wholeness and completeness in one's life
2. Sustaining: the ability to assist people to handle difficult times
3. Guiding: remove confusion, giving people a set of beliefs/standards to live by and trust
4. Reconciling: re-establishing broken relationships with the Lord and others
5. Nurturing: helping people sense security and affirmation within the Body of Christ

What is Christian Care Giving?

- Adjunct to pastoral ministry: helping someone with personal challenges and problems and to solve them as part of ongoing care and discipleship.
- Short term and focused care during a crisis to solve an immediate problem requiring biblical wisdom and common sense.
- To give healthy care to a new convert or struggling saint requires an understanding of human behavior consistent with the Christian world view and the teaching of God's word.
- Man was created perfect and whole in the very image of a personal Divine Creator.
- We are tripartite beings: body, soul, spirit and optimum health can only occur when a balance is obtained in all three areas of life.
- Every individual has an innate potential to be fulfilled. God has a wonderful plan for each person's life. Jesus was sent to be the provision for man.
  - (John 3:15-17: Rom 5:15-21; 1Cor 5:7)

- Redemption, reconciliation and regeneration provided by Christ's death must be personally received, in order to acquire the benefits from it. (John 3:1-15; Rom 10:9-17)
- Each person's experience is a "new birth" of God's life and essence within them.
- Spiritual growth is moving toward spiritual maturity. (Eph 4:15-24; Rom 6:11-23, Rom 12)

What makes Christian caregiving unique is the fact that the Bible is the final authority and standard of behavior for all. It is designed to assist people in understanding the Biblical concepts of growth and change.

Christian caregivers

- use both biblical insights and balanced understanding of human behavior.
- must depend on the power of the Holy Spirit to see lives changed.
- offer a way for people to deal with the hurts and traumas of their past. (Philippians 3:13-14)
- deal with the whole man, believing God through Jesus Christ and His atonement, brings total healing for the total man: spirit, soul and body.

Care Giving and the Need

- Caregiving ministry is discipleship and healing
  - 1 Corinthians 1
- Christians need to learn to comfort and correct
  - Galatians 6: bear with one another, nurture, and edify
- Most pastors are not specifically trained in giving counsel, yet all of them will counsel.
  - Will they counsel effectively? Impotently?
- Caregivers need to:
  - Have a personal, vibrant relationship with Jesus Christ
  - Be in relationship with the local church

- Have a proper attitude of heart
- Have God's wisdom
- Have knowledge; ministry training
- Not minister above their level of wholeness

A Divine Call

Some reject the idea that a divine call is considered necessary to enter the ministry. However, it is the only adequate foundation to build upon for success in this sacred vocation. All who are called to the ministry, especially to chaplaincy ministry, must sense they are called and have been chosen by God, and thus when properly equipped are well able to serve Christ through serving others through their chaplaincy service.

Regarding communication, you should enrich your vocabulary and speaking skills. Use words intelligently and accurately.

The Chaplain and His Church

A chaplain, living with purpose, will help his church and pastor to recapture the mission of the New Testament church. For this reason, the chaplains who are members of this organization should be of great help in all levels to their pastors.

> *"But I am the LORD thy God, that divided the sea, whose waves roared: The LORD of hosts is his name. And I have put my words in thy mouth, and I have covered thee in the shadow of mine hand, that I may plant the heavens, and lay the foundations of the earth, and say unto Zion, Thou art my people."*
>
> Isaiah 51:15-16

> *"Not slothful in business; fervent in spirit; serving the Lord;"*
>
> Romans 5:12

1. Being a chaplain is not a luxury but a commitment to God to serve inside and outside the community of Saints.
2. To serve others we must be diligent, that is, being prepared, alert, and ready to help.
3. In the vocabulary of the chaplain, the word "lazy" cannot exist.
4. Laziness is the enemy of spiritual passion.
5. Any service that we perform as chaplains must start by putting God as number one on our agenda, including all the work that we purpose to do.

Knowing Yourself and Understanding Others

First, to know ourselves and to understand others, it is very important that we continue the challenge that the Gospel makes to every Christian, to seek the full knowledge of his human condition according to the pattern God has given us in the person of Jesus Christ.

Nowadays, all of us who have prepared for ministry as pastors, lay leaders, evangelists, missionaries, teachers, and of course, as chaplains, need to know and understand that the therapeutic power of the Christian faith can not only reconcile brethren separated by stress, but can make them work together toward the high ideal, which is to proclaim the Gospel in order to achieve a better world by the will of God. The therapeutic power lies in the person of Jesus Christ and the Holy Spirit who has been sent to us.

In order to be a good chaplain, one must learn to listen. Especially in the days we live in when many people are depressed and have lost confidence, including spiritual leaders.

1. Witness - The chaplain must be a witness for Jesus Christ and not a social worker. Nowadays, we have many trained technicians in the things related to faith.
2. The Person of Jesus Christ – It is very important that Christ be integrated in the chaplain. It is better to be a good layman than a bad chaplain.

3. Communicating the Gospel – You must have great ability to communicate the gospel and know how to deal with the unbelievers.
4. Word and Actions - Whatever is conveyed in words must be backed up by actions.
5. Authority - Must have authority. Without authority there is no accountability. Authority comes from the Bible, which you ought to know and practice.
6. Leadership - A chaplain is expected to be a leader who has moral and spiritual authority. One who can guide in practical ways.
7. Faith - People admire those who believe and trust them to do great things. The chaplain should be primarily a person of faith.

The Chaplain's Behavior

Courtesy - The chaplain should be a polite person. His good habits and behavior should manifest abundantly as a representative of Christ.

"Love is patient, love is kind."

1 Corinthians 13:4 NIV

The apostle Paul urges us to be kind.

"Be kind and compassionate to one another, forgiving each other, just as in Christ God forgave you."

Ephesians 4:32 NIV

"Praise the LORD, for the LORD is good"

Psalm 135:3

The chaplain must follow the biblical counsel. To be a good chaplain, one must be led by the Word of God.

Good Vocabulary - In regard to communication, you should enrich your vocabulary and speaking skills. Use words intelligently and accurately.

Home - The chaplain's home must be exemplary. The chaplain should be a model in all things he does, especially in doing good works.

The Leader's Motivation

We must remember that demanding leadership challenges and leads to success. This is logical because people crave and want to give God their best. In this ministry, we believe God demands from us as chaplains, that we emphasize this type of leadership from the moment we arrived at this position. God has allowed us to understand that we are a movement, a Christian organization committed to a cause, namely, "Winning souls for the kingdom of heaven."

Maintain a Sense of Urgency

"Be very careful, then, how you live—not as unwise but as wise, making the most of every opportunity, because the days are evil."

Ephesians 5:15-16 NIV

The Apostle Paul advises the church to know how to make the most of time because the days are evil. In other words, to maintain a sense of urgency amidst the difficult days they were facing.

The Apostle Paul's advice: "Be very careful", implies a way of life, of attitudes and values. He is calling us to examine and evaluate our lives and our walk to ensure it is in harmony with God's, whom we serve.

His emphasis is that the Ephesians should have an awareness of God's revelation, the God whom they professed to serve. As chaplains we cannot ignore the times in which we live. My advice is, dear brethren, that we must keep that sense of urgency. Let's be diligent. We must give Christ and the study of His word top priority.

Appendix

Chaplain's Forms and Resources

(note: forms can be downloaded at
http://vision.edu/downloads/chaplain/forms.pdf)

CHAPLAIN'S ACTIVITY REPORT

Date Report Submitted _____ **Badge #** _____

Chaplains Name _____

Mentor/Supervisor _____

Report starting (date) _____ to _____

Activity # 1 Date _____

Type of Activity: ❑Service ❑ Prayer ❑ Counseling ❑ Bible Study ❑ Jail/Prison ❑Other

Accompanied by: (Pastor, Other Chaplain- Indicate Name and Title)

_____

How many people attended? _____ How many made a profession of faith: # _____

Name of Institution/Place of ministry activity and the address where it is located.

_____

_____

Describe Activity:

_____

_____

_____

Comments:

_____

_____

Activity # 2 Date _____

Type of Activity: ❏Service ❏ Prayer ❏ Counseling ❏ Bible Study ❏ Jail/Prison ❏Other

Accompanied by: (Pastor, Other Chaplain- Indicate Name and Title)

_____

How many people attended? _____ How many made a profession of faith: #_____

Name of Institution/Place of ministry activity and the address where it is located.

_____

_____

Describe Activity:

_____

_____

_____

Comments:

_____

_____

Activity # 3 Date _____

Type of Activity: ❑Service ❑ Prayer ❑ Counseling ❑ Bible Study ❑ Jail/Prison ❑Other

Accompanied by: (Pastor, Other Chaplain- Indicate Name and Title)

_____

How many people attended? _____ How many made a profession of faith: #_____

Name of Institution/Place of ministry activity and the address where it is located.

_____

_____

Describe Activity:

_____

_____

_____

Comments:

_____

_____

Activity # 4 Date _____

Type of Activity: ❏Service ❏ Prayer ❏ Counseling ❏ Bible Study ❏ Jail/Prison ❏Other

Accompanied by: (Pastor, Other Chaplain- Indicate Name and Title)

_____

How many people attended? _____ How many made a profession of faith: #_____

Name of Institution/Place of ministry activity and the address where it is located.

_____

_____

Describe Activity:

_____

_____

_____

Comments:

_____

_____

FUNERAL SERVICE PLANNING

Funeral director_____ Phone: _____ Facility:_____

Address: _____ City _____ State _____ Zip _____

Viewing? _____ Date of service: _____ Time: _____

Graveside Service: _____
_____

Family Contact: _____ Relationship: _____ Phone: _____
Address: _____ City _____ State _____ Zip _____

Family Contact: _____ Relationship: _____ Phone: _____
Address: _____ City _____ State _____ Zip _____

Deceased: _____ **Born:** Date _____ City _____ State _____

Died: Date _____ Place _____ City _____ State _____

Address: _____ City _____ State Zip _____

Survived by: (Spouse) _____ Married _____ (Children) _____
_____

(Parents) _____

(Siblings) _____

(Grandchildren) _____

(Great grandchildren) _____

Information surrounding the death: _____
_____
_____
_____
_____

Spiritual History: _____
_____
_____

Personal Data: (education, clubs, awards, sports, character, memorable moments) _____
_____
_____
_____
_____

Favorite songs _____

Favorite scriptures _____

Deceased's last words _____
_____
_____
_____
_____

Order of Service: (music, scripture, testimonies, etc.) _____
_____
_____
_____
_____

Meals for family & guests? _____
_____
_____
_____
_____

Flowers / Donations? _____
_____
_____
_____
_____
_____

Additional notes: _____
_____
_____
_____
_____
_____
_____
_____
_____
_____

FUNERAL SERVICE

I. **Introduction**

On behalf of the _____ family, I want to welcome you to this special <u>Memorial</u> service for _____, affectionately known to us all as "Mom." Before making my comments, let us pray.

II. **Regarding the Deceased**

We are here today to honor the life and memory of our wife, mother and friend, _____. First some comments on <u>Mom</u>.

_____ age _____, died _____, at <u>home</u>. <u>She</u> was born on _____, . (continue with reading of obituary)

_____ is survived by _____

III. **Eulogy**

Before continuing with the service, I want to give opportunity for anyone here today to make brief comments on _____.

- She Loved God
- She loved her family
- Singing of Blessed Assurance or other appropriate song.
- Details regarding this person's life that would be of interest to those attending. Tell her life story.

I. **Sermon- What Would <u>Mom</u> Say if She Were Here Today?**

What would <u>Mom</u> want to say to her loved ones and friends if she could speak today? I am certain she would make some important statements, to include:

- Her love for each of you
- Her hope for your future
- Her assurance that she is in a better place today
- Her desire that you make the kind of choices which will lead you to a life worth living, both now and for your eternity.

Certainly, the Word of God speaks to us of things eternal, and it would behoove us to look to the comfort of God's word as we consider the life of <u>Mom</u> and our lives as well. Remember,

Death is Universal, as seen in the following scriptures

"For we shall surely die and are like water spilled on the ground which cannot be gathered up again. Yet God does not take away life, but plans ways so that the banished one may not be cast out from him. "2 Sam. 14:14

"For he sees that even wise men die; the stupid and the senseless alike perish, and leave their wealth to others." Ps. 49: 10

" Therefore, just as through one man sin entered into the world, and death through sin, and so death spread to all men, because all sinned. "

"And inasmuch as it is appointed for men to die once and after this comes judgment." Heb. 9:27

Comment: Further...

Believers have a blessed hope

"For all have sinned and fall short of the glory of God." Rom. 3:23,

"The wages of sin is death, but the gift of God is eternal life, through Jesus Christ our Lord." Rom. 6:23,

For we know that
"God so loved the world that he gave his only son, that whosoever believes in him will not perish, but have everlasting life" Jn. 3:16

Precious in the eyes of the Lord are the death of his saints. Ps. 116:15

To be absent in the Body is to be present with the Lord. II Cor. 5:6
Since <u>Mom</u> gave her heart to the Lord, her sins were forgiven, and instead of the judgment of God she has received the blessings of eternal life in heaven with Christ. Thus, we have…

True Comfort, for again Jesus tells us

"Let not your heart be troubled; believe in God, believe also in me. In my Father's house are many dwelling places; if it were not so, I would have told you; I go to prepare a place for you. And if I go and prepare a place for you, I will come again, and receive you to myself; that where I am, there you may be also. And you know the way where I am going. Thomas said to him, Lord, we do not know where you are going, how do we know the way? Jesus said to him, I am the way, and the truth, and the life; no one comes to the father, but through me." Jn. 14:1-6

I am the resurrection and the Life, he who believes in me, though he be dead, yet shall he live. John 11: 25

As we consider the life of Mom, she would want us all to know that there is a way to life eternal, through Jesus. Let us pray.

Thank you for coming…

SERVICE FOR A CHILD

Viewing: _____ Service: _____

Music/Song: _____

Personal history: We are gathered here today to honor _____, born _____ in _____ He/she died _____

Name _____ is survived by: _____

_____

Poem: _____

Words from family and friends:

_____

- **God's promise of comfort in times of mourning**
  Matthew 5:4 (NIV) Blessed are those who mourn, for they will be comforted.

- **Comforted:** G3870 par-ak-al-eh '-o : to call near
  Matthew 5:4 (TMNT) "You're blessed when you feel you've lost what is most dear to you. Only then can you be embraced by the One most dear to you.

- **Jesus comforts his disciples as he speaks of his death John 14:27—29 (NIV)** Peace I leave with you; my peace I give you. I do not give to you as the world gives. Do not let your hearts be troubled and do not be afraid." You heard me say, 'I am going away and I am coming back to you.' If you loved me, you would be glad that I am going to the Father, for the Father is greater than I. 1 have told you now before it happens, so that when it does happen you will believe.

Angels at the time of death
- **Luke 16:19 - 23 (NASB)** "Now there was a rich man, and he habitually dressed in purple and fine linen, joyously living in splendor every day." And a poor man named Lazarus was laid at his gate, covered with sores, and longing to be fed with the crumbs which were falling from the rich man's table; besides, even the dogs were coming and licking his sores." Now the poor man died and was carried away by the angels to Abraham's bosom; and the rich man also died and was buried." In Hades he lifted up his eyes, being in torment,

We are encouraged to have an eternal perspective
- **2 Corinthians 4:18, 5:1-9 (NLT)** So we don't look at the troubles we can see right now; rather, we look forward to what we have not yet seen. For the troubles we see will soon be over, but the joys to come will last forever. For we know that when this earthly tent we live in is taken down—when we die and leave these bodies—we will have a home in heaven, an eternal body made for us by God himself and not by human hands. We grow weary in our present bodies, and we long for the day when we will put on our heavenly bodies like new clothing~ For we will not be spirits without bodies, but we will put on new heavenly bodies. Our dying bodies make us groan and sigh, but it's not that we want to die and have no bodies at all. We want to slip into our new bodies so that these dying bodies will be swallowed up by everlasting life. God himself has prepared us for this, and as a guarantee he has given us his Holy Spirit. So, we are always confident, even though we know that as long as we live in these bodies we are not at home with the Lord. That is why we live by believing and not by seeing. Yes, we are fully confident, and we would rather be away from these bodies, for then we will be at home with the Lord. So, our aim is to please him always, whether we are here in this body or away from this body.

We are comforted knowing that we will see those we love again at the return of the Lord Jesus Christ
- **1 Thessalonians 4:13 - 18 (NLT)** And now, brothers and sisters, I want you to know what will happen to the Christians who have died so you will not be full of sorrow like people who have no hope. 'For since we believe that Jesus died and was raised to life again, we also believe that when Jesus comes, God will bring back with Jesus all the Christians who have died.' I can tell you this directly from the Lord: We who are still living when the Lord returns will not rise to meet him ahead of those who are in their graves. 'For the Lord himself will come down from heaven with a commanding shout, with the call of the archangel, and with the trumpet call of God. First, all the Christians who have died will rise from their graves. 'Then, together with them, we who are still alive and remain on the earth will be caught up in the clouds to meet the Lord in the air and remain with him forever. So, comfort and encourage each other with these words.

Song: _____

Closing prayer: _____

WEDDING SERVICE

I. **Introduction**

I want to greet you on behalf of the bride, groom and their family and welcome you to this celebration. Each couple and each ceremony is unique and special, and this one is no different. This wedding celebration is also a time of reflection on what is important, even vital in life. _____ and _____ have determined in their hearts their desire to blend their lives in Holy Matrimony. Let us pray.

Who gives this woman to be wed?

II. **Addressing Bride and Groom**

We are here today to witness and join _____ and _____ at this sacred time. Let me first address the groom. _____, the Bible says that he who has found a wife has found a good thing and finds favor with the Lord. It has been the intention of God from the beginning for man to find his greatest human fulfillment in his wife and family.

Further, in Genesis 2 the word states that God recognized mankind's need, that it is not good for man to be alone. When the man first saw the woman in the garden he stated "this is bone of my bone and flesh of my flesh, she shall be called woman. For this cause a man shall leave his father and mother and cleave to his wife", to provide and protect, love and cherish. Your love is to be self-sacrificing, focused on her needs not just your own.

To You _____, the scripture states that both the man and woman were created equal by God, equal partners in terms of salvation and service, but uniquely different, with various roles and gifts. The wife is to honor and respect her husband, love and care for him, as would be done to the Lord.

With God's help, will you both commit to work on the fulfillment of each other's lives, if so, say

I do.

To the Witnesses, I was married 26 years before my first wife passed away. My wife and I had ups and downs like in any relationship, but we fulfilled the "until death do us part", by the grace of God, mutual commitment and hard work. My wife Karen and I had 26 wonderful years together in our journey and were equally committed to fulfilling each other by the Grace of God and mutual commitment. Faith and commitment is the glue that cemented our relationship. Relationships must grow and adapt, which takes much prayer, mercy, grace and work. It is worth the effort.

I. **VOWS**

Let us state our vows of covenant to one another, before these witnesses and Almighty God.

Face each other, take each other's hands, and repeat after me:

_____, do you take _____, to be your lawfully wedded wife, to love her, honor her, cherish and keep her, forsaking all others, as long as you both shall live? If so, say I do.

_____, do you take _____, to be your lawfully wedded husband, to honor him, love, support and nurture him, forsaking all others, as long as you both shall live? If so, say I do.

I. **RING CEREMONY**

(Take the rings, do hers first) _____, take _____ hand and place the ring on her finger. The ring is a symbol of the circle of eternal love and covenant that is not to be broken. _____ repeat after me… _____, receive this ring, as a pledge and token, of my faithfulness and wedded love.

_____, take _____ hand and place the ring on his finger. Again, the ring is a symbol of the circle of eternal love and covenant that is not to be broken. _____, repeat after me…. _____, receive this ring, as a pledge and token, of my faithfulness and wedded love.

II. **THE MESSAGE**

I saw a couple that had obviously been together for many many years. I would estimate they were well past the 50-year mark in marriage. As I observed them, my heart was filled with envy, tears coming to my eyes, as I saw in them the results of covenantal love worked out over many years

I do not know what their journey had been like, but I do know through good and bad times their love, etched on their weathered faces had grown deeper through adversity.

As I contemplated on what it must take to achieve the enviable position of this sexy couple, my thoughts settled on the wise words of the great man of God the Apostle Paul. May these words challenge, inspire and comfort you.

The Excellence of Love

1. If I speak with the tongues of men and of angels, but do not have love, I have become a noisy gong or a clanging cymbal.
2. If I have the gift of prophecy, and know all mysteries and all knowledge; and if I have all faith, so as to remove mountains, but do not have love, I am nothing.
3. And if I give all my possessions to feed the poor, and if I surrender my body to be burned, but do not have love, it profits me nothing.
4. Love is patient, love is kind and is not jealous; love does not brag and is not arrogant,
5. Love does not act unbecomingly; it does not seek its own, is not provoked, does not take into account a wrong suffered,
6. Love does not rejoice in unrighteousness, but rejoices with the truth;
7. Love bears all things, believes all things, hopes all things, and endures all things.
8. Love never fails; but if there are gifts of prophecy, they will be done away; if there are tongues, they will cease; if there is knowledge, it will be done away.
9. For we know in part and we prophesy in part;
10. But when the perfect comes, the partial will be done away.
11. When I was a child, I used to speak like a child, think like a child, reason like a child; when I became a man, I did away with childish things.
12. For now we see in a mirror dimly, but then face to face; now I know in part, but then I will know fully just as I also have been fully known.
13. But now faith, hope, love, abide these three; but the greatest of these is love.

RULES AND REGULATIONS

Regulation: *Law, rule principle, to govern the system, a company or organization.*

1. In the event of removal, you quit or are discharged from the Organization; you will not be reconsidered for membership without due process and evaluation.
2. Obey all rules and regulations of the organization.
3. Obey all rules and institutional regulations.
4. Maintain a good testimony.
5. Do not use the credentials if you're under discipline in your church.
6. In the event of a breach of the law, the officers of this organization must be notified immediately.
7. You will be dismissed if convicted of any crime.
8. You will be removed from ministry for giving false information.
9. Dress appropriately.
10. Report to this organization of the work being done.
11. Identify yourself adequately as necessary or required.
12. Use the ID plate properly.
13. Use the ID plate and your identification together.
14. Do not lend your ID plate or identification to anyone.
15. Do not confuse our credentials with any other.
16. Do not alter the credentials.
17. Do not try to use our credentials for public transportation.
18. If you lose your credentials, you must report it promptly.
19. Do not abuse the position or authority you've been given to exercise.

MEMBER INFORMATION UPDATE FORM

We need to update our records. Please provide the information requested and complete full address including apartment number and zip code, telephone number and area code. Please write above the line provided for that use. Thank you.

NAME _____ **Badge No.** _____

    Title: Full Name: First   Middle   Last

STREET ADDRESS

_____

Street Name, Ave. or St.   *Apartment #*   *County*   *State*   *Zip Code*

MAILING ADDRESS IF DIFFERENT   CHECK "SAME AS ABOVE ADDRESS"

_____

Address or PO BOX Number   *County,*   *State*   *Zip Code*

TELEPHONES:

_____

_ *Home (Include area code)*   *Job (Optional)*   *Cell Phone*

CHURCH INFORMATION:

_____

   Pastor's Name   *Church Name*   *Church Address*

MINISTRY INFORMATION:

_____

   Ministry Name   *Address/PO Box*   *City, State*   *Zip Code*

Ministry Telephone   Fax   Email

_____ I Need My Id Renewed   Expiration Date: _____

_____ I Wish To Resign From The Chaplaincy And Am Returning My Id And Badge.

(Enclosed Id and Badge – Required).

You May Give an Explanation

_____
_____
_____
_____
_____
_____
_____
_____
_____
_____
_____
_____

*PLEASE ATTACH A REPORT OF ALL CHAPLAIN ACTIVITIES FOR THE PAST YEAR.

About the Author/Editor

Dr. Stan DeKoven is the International President of Vision International University, and Founder/President of the Vision International Training and Education Network. Vision/VITEN specializes in establishing and supporting local, Church-based Bible Colleges and distance education programs. Through their unique "Bible College in a Box" system, they are presently serving more than 4,000 Resource Centers in over 150 countries and over 100,000 students through its affiliated ministries.

Stan has a diverse background in Education, Business, Military, Leadership, and Counseling. He has pioneered two very successful businesses while consulting with others nationally and internationally. Stan has earned a bachelor's degree in Psychology from San Diego State University, a master's degree in Counseling from Webster University, a Doctor of Ministry degree from Evangelical Theological Seminary and a Doctor of Philosophy in Counseling Psychology from the Professional School of Psychological Studies. Dr. DeKoven holds credentials in School Psychology, Marriage and Family Therapy, and clinical membership in many professional organizations.

He specializes in Leadership development, and assisting executives achieve their potential in the marketplace. He is also an Executive Coaching Specialist for The Vision Group, and the founder of Walk in Wisdom media ministries.

He is a licensed Marriage and Family Therapist in the State of California with over 35 years of professional services, specializing in:

Crisis Ministry
Domestic Violence and Recovery
Substance Abuse Treatment
General Family problems with children and Teens

Personal Coaching for men and women seeking improvement in vocation or relationship

Books by Dr. DeKoven

Crisis Counseling
Family Violence: Patterns of Destruction
Substance Abuse Therapy
Kingdom Quest: The Journey to Wholeness
New Beginnings: A Sure Foundation
Marriage and Family Life
On Belay! An Introduction to Christian Counseling
Group Dynamics
I Want to Be Like You, Dad: Breaking Free and Discovering the Father's Heart
Grief Relief
Parenting on Purpose
Old & New Testament Surveys
Fresh Manna (How to Study the Bible)
Leadership in the Church: In the Eye of the Storm
Visionary Leadership
Prelude to a Requiem: Principles of Leadership from the Upper Room
Supernatural Architecture (The Apostolic Church of 21st Century & Beyond)
And 20+ more books and booklets in various topics, see at www.booksbyvision.org

Dr Stan speaks on a wide range of topics from Christian Business, Christian Counseling, Leadership, Team Dynamics, Personal Coaching, Church Consultancy, Setting up Local Church Counseling, Teaching and Mission Ministries, World & Urban Missions, Youth, Church Structure and Personal and Corporate Vision.

Dr Stan assists many younger ministers develop in ministry. Through speaking and consulting, he gives relational oversight to churches both nationally and internationally. As such, he is in demand around the globe to speak in Leadership Conferences and to teach in Bible Colleges/Universities.

To schedule speaking or contact the author:
Vision International University: www.vision.edu
Walk in Wisdom Ministries: www.drstandekoven.com
Or call 760-789-4700

www.ingramcontent.com/pod-product-compliance
Lightning Source LLC
Chambersburg PA
CBHW071721090426
42738CB00009B/1842